SLURP ON.

Instant RAMEN Kitchen

Instant RAMEN Kitchen

40+ Delicious Recipes That Go Beyond the Packet

PETER J. KIM

Photographs by BOBBI LIN

CHRONICLE BOOKS

SAN FRANCISCO

Library of Congress Cataloging-in-Publication Data

Names: Kim, Peter J. author | Lin, Bobbi photographer
Title: Instant ramen kitchen : 40+ delicious recipes that go beyond the packet / Peter J. Kim ; photography by Bobbi Lin.
Description: San Francisco : Chronicle Books, [2025] | Includes index.
Identifiers: LCCN 2025010167 | ISBN 9781797225586 hardcover
Subjects: LCSH: Ramen | LCGFT: Cookbooks
Classification: LCC TX809.N65 K563 2025 | DDC 641.82/2--dc23/eng/20250319
LC record available at https://lccn.loc.gov/2025010167

Manufactured in China.

Photographs by Bobbi Lin.
Photographs on pages 19 through 21 courtesy of Nissin Food Products.
Photographs on pages 59 through 63 by Ryan Cunningham.
Food styling by Fanny Pan.
Food styling assistance by Alison Fellion.
Design and illustrations by Wynne Au-Yeung.

7UP is a registered trademark of Dr Pepper/Seven Up, Inc. Buldak is a registered trademark of Samayang Foods Inc. Chapagetti, Neoguri, Shin Black, and Shin Ramyum are registered trademarks of Nong Shim Co., Ltd. Frank's RedHot is a registered trademark of The French's Food Company LLC. Jin Mild and Jin Spicy are registered trademarks of Ottogi Corporation. La Choy is a registered trademark of Conagra G&S (CAG), LLC. M&M's is a registered trademark of Mars, Incorporated. Maruchan is a registered trademark of Maruchan, Inc. Microplane is a registered trademark of Grace Manufacturing, Inc. Sapporo Ichiban is a registered trademark of Sanyo Shokuhin Kabushiki Kaisha. Sriracha is a registered trademark of J&P Park Acquisitions, Inc. Tapatío is a registered trademark of Tapatio Foods, LLC. Top Ramen is a registered trademark of Nissin Foods Holdings Co., Ltd.

10 9 8 7 6 5 4 3 2 1

Chronicle books and gifts are available at special quantity discounts to corporations, professional associations, literacy programs, and other organizations. For details and discount information, please contact our premiums department at corporategifts@chroniclebooks.com or at 1-800-759-0190.

Chronicle Books LLC
680 Second Street
San Francisco, California 94107
www.chroniclebooks.com

Contents

PART I

Welcome to the Instant Ramen Kitchen

Introduction

My Instant Ramen

Many cookbooks start with romantic childhood memories. You know: grandma's made-from-scratch dumplings, fresh fruit plucked from the family garden, the intoxicating aromas wafting out of the stockpot, and so on.

Nope—not this book. Most of *my* childhood food memories wafted out of the microwave. My parents were immigrant entrepreneurs who hustled day and night to sell birthday cards and Precious Moments at our family Hallmark store. They cooked when they could, but more often than not, I was on my own for dinner. On those evenings, I'd pop a Kid Cuisine frozen dinner, Dinty Moore beef stew, or Hot Pocket in the microwave and dig in while watching TV. (To this day, canned beef stew over white rice is one of my comfort foods.)

One dish stood out because it actually got me cooking: instant ramen. Even though I was otherwise useless in the kitchen, I knew how to heat a pot of water, drop in the noodle cake and seasoning sachet, wait a few minutes, and then pour the whole mess into a big bowl.

I can actually remember my very first bite of instant ramen. It was a packet of original-flavored Sapporo Ichiban. I was a young child in the Midwest, and I'd never seen anything like it. I sat at a table in my kitchen and took in the aromas as I looked at the unassuming bowl of brown soup. But—oof—I can recall the sensation of tasting it for the first time. Slippery, chewy noodles enrobed in a heady broth rich with umami and the flavors of soy sauce and chicken. A salty, savory, oniony flavor that lingered in my mouth. I ate the noodles in a fervor and then tipped the bowl to my mouth to finish off the broth. I knew this would be far from my last bowl of instant ramen.

Soon after, my mom showed me the time-honored Korean tradition of cracking an egg directly into the simmering soup, giving it a twirl with chopsticks, and then finishing it off with a sprinkle of sliced scallions. This made an already delicious dish even more complete. The egg fortified the broth with its hearti- ness, and the scallion added a welcome green, pungent note.

As is the case for many instant ramen eaters, I came to realize that the possibilities extended well beyond eggs and scallions. Sliced hot dogs, frozen broccoli, dumplings, leftover Korean banchan side dishes—all of it could come together with the instant ramen and make a delicious meal. As someone who had previously only known how to cook Kraft mac 'n' cheese, the notion of having choices in the kitchen was a novel one. Imagine that: I didn't need to follow a recipe! I could follow my nose and my intuition to improvise each bowl. As I tiptoed my way through the different possibilities, each bowl I made was different and, surprisingly, consistently delicious. Instant ramen proved to be a forgiving partner for my culinary experimentation. It seemed to always turn out well, no matter what I flung at it.

This was the beginning of a lifelong obsession with creative instant ramen cookery. I almost never made instant ramen au naturel, with no tweaks or additions. Instead, each packet of instant ramen was a chance to try something new.

Instant ramen planted a seed of culinary creativity that blossomed into broader kitchen experimentation. By the time I was sixteen, I was cooking jambalaya, rolling out fresh pasta sheets, and tinkering with developing recipes of my own. I came up with a steak recipe that became a go-to dish whenever my parents were entertaining guests. (It was a bulgogi-marinated New York strip steak topped with cilantro and lime and served with coconut rice.)

Later in life, I spent several years abroad and had the opportunity to discover food traditions around the world. I pounded fufu in Cameroon, scooped up kitfo in Ethiopia, tasted freshly pressed olive oil in Jordan, snacked on jars of pickled peppers in Romania, and fired up paella in the streets of Valencia, Spain. I went on to complete a certificate program at the French Culinary Institute, after which I led the creation of the Museum of Food and Drink, a nonprofit that explores the intersection of food and culture. All of this started with instant ramen.

It's no exaggeration to say that my culinary identity has been built on a foundation of noodle cakes and seasoning sachets. It's a dish that delighted me as a child, inspired me as a nascent cook, and grew with me as I built a career in food. All along, as I tinkered with instant ramen, it wasn't just the noodles that evolved—I did too. With this book, I hope to help you find the same kind of inspiration in those little wavy fried noodles.

Rethinking Instant Ramen

By now, I have consumed thousands of bowls of instant ramen. I half-jokingly wonder just how many molecules in my body I can attribute to the stuff. And I continue to eat it regularly—I can't get enough of it.

I'm not the only one, either. According to the World Instant Noodles Association, Americans consumed 5.15 billion servings of instant ramen in 2022. You can find it stocked in super-markets and convenience stores worldwide. And yet, despite its popularity, many people have a dismissive attitude toward instant ramen. "Oh, it's cheap-o processed 'junk food.'" "It's for starving college students." (The starving student line, in partic-ular, is so common it's become a tired cliché. Let's please put that line to bed.) I reject that characterization. Instant ramen deserves our respect.

For starters, it's a dish that has a direct lineage from tradi-tional ramen, which itself, by some accounts, has a history that stretches back for centuries to the introduction of Chinese noodles to Japan. And for billions of people in countries around the world, instant ramen is not "dorm food." It's food food. In India, Maggi noodles have a vaunted place in the pantry. In Nigeria, Indomie instant ramen is so popular that the word *Indomie* has become synonymous with "noodles." In Mexico, one national newspaper declared the country "Maruchan Nation." To understand the dish's place in Korean culture, you can turn to the movie screen. Instant ramen appears everywhere in Korean films. In the 2019 film *Parasite*, a family returns home from a trip, and the first thing they want to eat is "Chapaguri," a mash-up of Chapagetti and Neoguri, two brands of instant ramen. In the film, it's made with the addition of beef in under 8 minutes. This scene prompted an internet craze and countless videos of people making the dish.

My family is proudly a part of the global instant ramen fan club. With my parents, it's a comforting ritual. Once we've decided to have it as a meal, the next steps unfold on autopilot: fill a pot with water, grab vegetables and a few eggs out of the fridge, and pick out an instant ramen brand from the pantry—usually it's Shin Ramyun or Neoguri in our case. Even though it's a meal we've had many times, it's still met each time with genuine enthusiasm. With my kids, instant ramen is one of the few sure-fire meals that they'll *always* be up for eating. This is no small feat considering the fact that my daughter vehemently rejects 90 percent of the food presented to her.

There's a reason why instant ramen has become such a beloved facet of so many families and food cultures. It uniquely sits at the intersection of easy and delicious.

On the ease front, can anything beat it? It isn't called *instant* for nothing. If you can reach the stovetop, you can make instant ramen, even if you've never cooked a thing in your life. On the deliciousness front, it has flavors that appeal to eaters across the spectrum. While it's something that certainly appeals to the masses, it's a dish that top chefs will happily enjoy too. I've been to high-end culinary industry parties where both caviar and cup ramen were served. When something tastes good, it tastes good—and all the better if it's cheap.

Taken together, these qualities give instant ramen its superpower: it is a culinary turbocharger. With instant ramen, even a novice cook can make something delicious that would satisfy a Michelin-starred chef. How beautiful is that?

This superpower is what makes instant ramen such a powerful tool to unlock creativity. It is a blank canvas, ready to embrace any condiment, vegetable, or protein you want to throw at it. It's hard to take a wrong turn because the contents of the instant ramen packet contain enough flavor and seasoning to all but guarantee deliciousness. With instant ramen, you can let go of your inhibitions and focus on the fun and creativity of cooking, rather than fussing over whether it'll work at all.

The possibilities extend well beyond East Asian cuisines. As you'll see in this book, with just a few tweaks, you can turn a packet of instant ramen into dishes inspired by creamy Brazilian moqueca, bright red Ukrainian borscht, or even Italian aglio e olio.

So, let's start giving instant ramen the respect it deserves. It's easy, affordable, and versatile. It's a central part of many cultural identities. And, as this book will show, it can enable you to cook with confidence, tap into your culinary creativity, and make some seriously delicious food.

A Product of History and Ingenuity

In 2000, the Fuji Research Institute conducted a poll of two thousand residents of the Kanto region of Japan, which includes Tokyo, asking them to name the greatest Japanese invention of the twentieth century. The overwhelming winner? You guessed it: instant ramen. The packaged noodles won out over karaoke, the Walkman, home computer consoles, compact discs, and even Pokémon. It's easy to understand why—instant ramen has influenced diets around the world.

Its origins lie with Japanese inventor Momofuku Ando, who created the world's first successful instant ramen, Chicken Ramen, in 1958. Though historian George Solt has pointed out that there may have been other unsuccessful instant ramens prior to Chicken Ramen's debut, ultimately, we owe the global phenomenon that is instant ramen as we know it today to Ando's innovation and vision.

Chicken Ramen was as much a product of Ando's ingenuity as it was of Japan's economic climate in the aftermath of World War II. Many Japanese people struggled in poverty and relied on food aid from the United States, much of which consisted of American-grown wheat, which led to a rise in the consumption of wheat-based noodles. As the story goes, soon after the end of the war, Ando witnessed a long line of hungry people waiting to eat ramen at a temporary stall in Osaka, a scene that later inspired him to try to create a more accessible form of ramen.

After much experimentation, he developed a technique for deep-frying noodles that simultaneously made them slow to spoil and fast to cook. This formed the basis for a product that was delicious, safe, convenient, affordable, and nonperishable and took advantage of the broad availability of wheat. In 1971, Ando followed up with the invention of Cup Noodles, further expanding the popularity of instant ramen. Today, Ando's company, Nissin Foods, is a global business and is one of many companies producing instant ramen for consumers around the world.

With so much variety, what actually defines instant ramen? There are two common components in all instant ramen: a dried, quick-cooking noodle cake (usually fried, but sometimes air-dried) and a seasoning sachet used to create a soup or sauce. Some instant ramen brands include additional components such as dried vegetable flakes or flavored oils.

The content of a packet of instant ramen mimics the components of traditional ramen, a soup noodle dish considered by many to be a cornerstone of Japanese food culture. Most traditional ramen dishes share three components: noodles, soup, and toppings. The noodles are made from wheat and alkaline minerals called *kansui*, which give the noodles their distinctive flavor and texture—as well as the ability to stay chewy even when immersed in a hot liquid. The soup is made from two subcomponents: tare, a concentrated sauce, and broth made from meat, bones, vegetables, and seaweed. Traditional ramen toppings vary immensely from restaurant to restaurant, but common ones include flavored oils and fats, chashu (soy-marinated pork belly), jammy eggs, sliced scallions, and menma (seasoned bamboo shoots).

While instant ramen and traditional ramen have similar frameworks, they differ significantly in many other ways. Traditional ramen-making is an artisanal craft where broths are simmered and adjusted over many hours, top-quality ingredients are prized, and chefs express their creativity through balancing and combining flavors in novel ways. Instant ramen is, in many ways, the opposite: it's made in factories, it uses economical ingredients, and it can be made in minutes with consistent results that have been precisely calibrated by the manufacturer. Both can be delicious.

Instant Ramen Kitchen bridges the gap, bringing together the best of both worlds: the speed and ease of instant ramen with a methodology that opens the door to the creativity and flavor possibilities of traditional ramen.

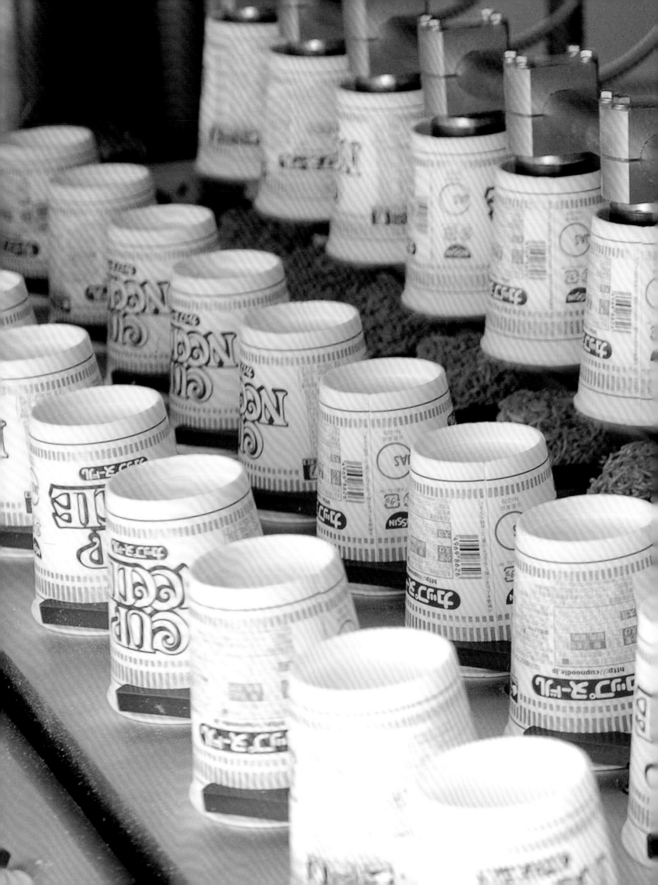

TRADITIONAL TOKYO RAMEN

INSTANT SHIN RAMYUN

Noodles

Wheat flour noodles with kansui, alkaline minerals that provide chew and springiness

Wheat flour and potato starch noodles with kansui, deep-fried in palm oil for a long shelf life and to create a porous structure that cooks quickly

Toppings

Varies, but may include chashu pork, bean sprouts, bamboo shoots, fish cakes, sliced scallions, and a jammy egg

Dried vegetable sachet includes bok choy, shiitake mushrooms, carrot, green onion, and red chile

Soup

A savory stock made from long-simmered chicken bones and umami-rich seaweed, with tare (a concentrated sauce) made from soy sauce

Beef extracts, umami-rich flavor enhancers, and other powdered ingredients, including garlic, chile, and soy sauce

The Power of Improvisation

Food and music have always been pillars in my life. Recently, I've increasingly seen an interconnectedness between food and music, a revelation that helped inspire this book. Allow me to explain.

I've been a lifelong musician. I learned violin and piano at a young age, and, as an adolescent, I taught myself to play guitar and sing. I developed a deep appreciation for a wide world of music, including the harmonies of Bach, the soulfulness of Nina Simone, the complexity of Radiohead, and the musicality of Stevie Wonder. Over the years, I enjoyed playing their tunes by mimicking recordings or working off of sheet music.

A little while ago, I started to join musical jam sessions. One musician would start playing a hook or chord progression to kick things off. From there, anything would go. Sometimes the song would evolve in a predictable way; other times it would take unexpected turns. This felt entirely different from how I'd approached music previously. At first, the unpredictable nature of a jam terrified me whenever I took the microphone to sing. My nervousness was so intense that I'd actually feel a painful knot in my stomach that would continue for hours after the jam ended.

Indeed, sometimes my performance was mediocre at best. However, other times, I reached a state of total connection with the other musicians and, together, we weaved a soundscape in real time. Improvisational music is wholly different from playing a known song. From a process standpoint, it requires being present, listening, interacting with the music, and tapping into your creative spirit. Most importantly, you feel *free*, able to choose where you're going rather than mechanically following directions. The output feels special and unique, because it is. While playing sheet music is certainly expressive, jamming is far more creative.

I've come to realize the same thing applies to cooking. Sure, you can follow recipes to a T and enjoy plenty of nice meals that way. But nothing can compare to the sheer pleasure and magical feeling of improvising a meal based on the ingredients you have on hand. Whatever you make, if you "jam" your way through making it, it'll feel special and uniquely *you*.

Aside from the pleasure of cooking this way, it's practically useful. Once you've become comfortable with improvis-ing, you won't feel constrained by ingredient lists in recipes. You can craft a meal out of whatever is in your refrigerator and pantry. You can spot a perfect-looking vegetable in the farmers' market and build a meal around it.

If you're the kind of person who only follows recipes or doesn't cook at all, how can you get started with improvising? This is where instant ramen, and this book, come in. I've found that instant ramen is an exceptionally powerful tool to empower culinary improvisation for a few reasons:

- **It's reliably delicious.** The seasoning sachet provides a solid foundation of salt, umami, and aromatics. This takes a lot of the guesswork out of cooking and you can focus on following your creative spirit, adding whatever ingredients feel right, knowing it will probably taste great. On top of that, the noodles provide a backbone of calories that ensure your final dish is nourishing. Together, instant ramen acts like a friendly flotation device that lets you dive into improvisation without fear.

- **It's versatile.** While you might think of instant ramen as being an Asian dish, it can actually take on the flavors of nearly any cuisine.

- **It's cheap and fast.** The cost of failure is low. Even if it doesn't work out (which is unlikely), you will only be out a couple of bucks and 15 minutes. This means you can just try again right away.

How to Use This Book

Actually, please don't think of *Instant Ramen Kitchen* as a cookbook.

A cookbook is like a signposted path. It tells you exactly where to go, step by step. Instead, think of this book as a guide. It's meant to show you the general lay of the land and some points of interest. My intention is to help you chart your own path in the kitchen as you discover the joy of improvisational cooking.

I'll share a methodology and mindset that I've developed over the decades in cooking with instant ramen. When I do this for myself, I do it casually without using any timers or measuring utensils. I don't follow any recipes. I peruse my kitchen, find some ingredients, and pull it all together on the fly.

However, in this book, contradictory to my own everyday cooking, my method includes a lot of precise measurements and timing, and the recipes—like all recipes—call for specific ingredients. I don't mean for this to be intimidating or restrictive. Think of it as a handrail until you're ready to strike off on your own, using your own intuitive sense for how to cook.

Perhaps you've had the experience of asking someone how they cooked something, only to receive a response along the lines of, "Oh, a pinch of this, a handful of that." It may accurately reflect that person's approach to the recipe, but it's quite unhelpful for someone who wants to learn how to make it.

JUMPING IN

If you want to jump right into things without reading through the method first, here are two ways to do it.

Start with your ingredients. Flip to the Instant Flavor Bank chapter (page 66). Based on what you already have in your refrigerator and pantry, pick out an ingredient or two. Cook up a bowl of instant ramen using these ingredients.

Start with a recipe. A few good, easy options that use common ingredients are Basic Ramen (page 145), Tomato and Egg Stir-Fry Ramen (page 171), Frijoles de la Ollu Ramon (page 180), and Aglio e Olio Ramen (page 217).

So, at first, you may want to use my exact specifications to get the hang of things. Then, please feel free to toss aside the guidance and do what feels right. These recipes are templates, meant to be reworked and reimagined. Guess at the timing. Eyeball the measurements. Start taking baby steps with your improvisation by making little substitutions. Use ground chicken instead of ground beef, basil instead of cilantro, fennel seed instead of cumin, cauliflower instead of broccoli.

As you grow more confident, take a look around your kitchen and pick any ingredient you see, even if it seems counter-intuitive. It could be yesterday's leftovers, a rarely used spice, veggies you happen to have on hand, or an open can of beans—whatever it might be, take a look at my guidance in the Instant Flavor Bank chapter, then drop it in and taste what happens.

The beauty of working with instant ramen is that it's hard to make anything that is *not* delicious. Relax and enjoy the ride.

The Method

Breaking Things Down

Imagine being able to walk into your kitchen and whip up a flavorful, beautiful bowl of noodles in under 10 minutes flat. It's possible with instant ramen.

When you hear a professional musician perform a tune, it comes out as a polished whole, one part seamlessly flowing into another. However, behind the scenes, that musician probably learned that tune by playing it slowly, breaking it down into sections, and working methodically from one to the next.

Similarly, if you watched me cook with instant ramen, it'd look like one fluid process: ingredients get chopped up and thrown in, noodles get simmered, and then in a matter of minutes, a steaming bowl of ramen is ready to eat. If you zoomed in on the process, though, you'd find that there are a surprising number of techniques and knowledge that come into play to make the magic happen.

Don't worry—it's all quite accessible and easy to learn. But to get there, just like learning a song, it's helpful to break down the process, step by step. At first glance, this may seem like a lot of information to take in. However, by learning this method, you're not just learning how to cook instant ramen—you're learning how to cook, period. All of the techniques in my method are entirely applicable to general cooking.

As I mentioned earlier, you don't need to master this method before cooking. Feel free to jump right in, try a recipe, and try improvising using the Instant Flavor Bank as a reference. Over time, it's worth investing the effort to learn the method. You will be even better equipped to build interesting and delicious flavor profiles in instant ramen—and in anything you cook. Soon enough, you'll be zipping around the kitchen whipping up dishes just like a top musician burning through a jazz tune.

Equipment

Having the right equipment will help you achieve the best results. The one thing that will make a big difference is having the right-size saucepan. If your saucepan is too big, the liquid level will be too low to properly cook your noodles. If your saucepan is too small, you'll have to break up noodle cakes to get them to fit, which means shorter, less satisfying noodles. Beyond that, don't fret too much. If you have a bowl and a fork or chopsticks, you have enough to get started.

2-cup [475 ml] measuring cup
The perfect tool for measuring out liquids to add to your ramen.

Chopsticks
Ditch the plastic ones. Stick to wooden chopsticks for an optimal grip.

Kitchen timer
Certain aspects of instant ramen—especially cooking the noodles—are sensitive to timing. Your phone's timer is a good option, but it's nice to have a dedicated timer so you're not fumbling for your phone in the kitchen.

Medium saucepan
(about a 2-quart [1.9 L] volume)
This allows space for your ingredients while minimizing splashing. You also want to make sure it's wide enough to fit a noodle cake, which can be as wide as 6½ inches [16.5 cm]. A fitted lid is good for splatter protection when making thicker soups or sauces.

Prep bowls

Some 6- to 8-ounce [170 to 225 ml] bowls are perfect to help organize your ingredients. It may mean you have a few extra dishes to wash, but having things portioned in bowls makes cooking a more pleasant, seamless experience (especially if you are nervous in the kitchen).

Spider strainer

Great for making Jammy Eggs (page 160) and for lifting noodles out of the pot. A slotted spoon can also do the trick.

Spoon

A Japanese-style soupspoon, with its flat bottom and large capacity, is ideal for scooping up the perfect bite.

The Four Phases

I've found it helpful to conceptualize the instant ramen cooking process as having four phases: (1) the Prep, (2) the Pre-Simmer, (3) the Simmer, and (4) the Finish. Like a relay race, each phase uniquely contributes to your final dish.

② PRE-SIMMER

ACTIONS: Sear, sauté, bloom, and infuse
GOALS: Brown and extract flavor

① PREP

ACTIONS: Slice and measure
GOALS: Prepare to cook

④ FINISH

③ SIMMER

ACTIONS: Mix, top, and serve

GOALS: Add fresh ingredients, plate ramen

ACTION: Simmer

GOALS: Cook noodles and ingredients

All the ramen recipes in this book are labeled with these phases, with the exception of the Prep phase. I assume that the Prep phase happens while you are getting your ingredients together.

① Prep

In the Prep phase you have one goal: prepare all the ingredients and equipment you need to start cooking.

Preparing ingredients ahead of time is a good practice, no matter what you're cooking. One mistake home cooks often make is bouncing back and forth frenetically between grabbing ingredients, prepping them, and cooking them. This can lead to chaos in the kitchen: food scorching while you have your head in the refrigerator, ingredients going tumbling to the floor as you hurriedly shuttle them over to the stovetop, or smacking your forehead when you realize you forgot to add a key ingredient at the beginning. This is especially true for instant ramen. Because it only takes a few minutes to cook, some steps can come down to a matter of seconds.

Additionally, one way to increase your speed in the kitchen is to group related actions together. It's much more efficient to peel, peel, peel, then chop, chop, chop, and then move to cooking, rather than peel, chop, cook, peel, chop, cook.

In the culinary industry, this preparation is called the *mise en place*, which can be translated as "everything in its place." Even though this is something done at restaurants, it's a good practice for home cooks at any level. Good preparation allows you to cook your instant ramen at lightning speed, without any hiccups.

Here's a checklist of things to do during this phase.

- **Pick your ingredients.** If you're following a recipe, you'll want to ensure you have everything on the ingredients list, including any substitutions or additions you'd like to make. If you are improvising, this means taking a second to look in your refrigerator and pantry, pulling out what you plan to use, and getting it ready to go.

- **Cut ingredients down to size.** Cooking large-size ingredients is simply not an option for instant ramen—they take too long, which defeats the purpose of these noodles.

- **Measure out all your ingredients.** I prefer to keep each one measured out in its own bowl. But if that sounds like a hassle, you can at least keep your cut vegetables in piles on your cutting board and line up any containers or bottles that you'll use.

- **Lay out all equipment.** Pull out any measuring spoons and cups, tongs, or other tools, as well as your ramen bowl, chopsticks, and spoon.

- **Measure your liquids.** Whether it's just water, water and milk, or any other combination of liquids, have them measured out and ready to be added.

- **Open your package of instant ramen and pull out the noodle cake and seasoning sachet.** I can't tell you the number of times I've been in a rush and fumbled opening a package of instant ramen, sending noodles skittering to the ground. It may seem like a no-brainer, but you can ensure a smoother execution by taking a second to open the package ahead of time.

- **Start a kitchen timer.** You'll notice that I've indicated some precise timing in my process. With practice, you'll be able to wing it once you've developed your intuition in the kitchen. Until then, keep an eye on time by setting a timer that is running constantly while you cook. A stopwatch that counts up from zero is ideal, but if your timer only counts down, you can set it for, say, 30 minutes, which is more than enough time to complete a recipe.

Once you're ready to go, it's time to put a saucepan on your stovetop, turn it on, and get cooking.

BREAKING THE CAKE

For the most part, I recommend keeping the noodle cake intact, which results in longer noodles and, to me, more fun slurping. However, there are several reasons you may want to break up the noodle cake. For one, a smaller noodle cake is easier to manipulate in the saucepan, especially if it's crowded with other ingredients. Additionally, a smaller noodle size may be more appropriate for certain dishes. For example, if you're making mac 'n' cheese with instant ramen, you may prefer having smaller noodles that more closely mimic the mouthfeel of elbow macaroni. If you're making a soup, tiny broken-up noodles allow it to be eaten solely with a spoon, without the need for chopsticks.

If you're just breaking the noodle cake in half or quarters, you can do that with your hands over the saucepan. If you're breaking it into smaller pieces, crush the noodle cake with your hands inside the instant ramen packet before opening it. In this case, it helps to first poke a small hole in the package to keep it from popping open.

② Pre-Simmer

Now that your saucepan is heating up, you've officially entered the Pre-Simmer phase. This phase encompasses everything you'll do up to adding liquids and noodles to the saucepan.

This is the phase for dry-cooking methods, which do not involve the use of liquids (other than fats) and are foundational methods for any cook to have in their repertoire. During this phase, you have two goals:

1 Develop flavor through browning.

2 Extract flavor from your ingredients by cooking them in fat.

There are quite a few dry-cooking methods, including roasting, broiling, and grilling. For instant ramen cookery, the four most useful methods are searing, sautéing, blooming, and infusing. While all four of these methods serve both goals, searing and sautéing are focused on browning, and blooming and infusing are focused on flavor extraction.

> **SKIP THE PRE-SIMMER**
>
> Why might you forgo the Pre-Simmer phase and add ingredients at the Simmer phase without browning them first? One reason is speed. The more ingredients you try to sear, the longer it will take to brown them—you may have heard the old adage "Don't crowd the pan." Another reason is flavor or appearance. You may prefer the cleaner look and taste of ingredients that have only been simmered without browning. This is an opportunity to experiment with your own preferences.

HOW BROWNING MAKES FOOD DELICIOUS

Dry cooking allows you to cook at high temperatures that can brown food to develop delicious flavors. By contrast, simmering water maxes out at 212°F [100°C] (the boiling point of water), which is generally not hot enough to brown food.

When you brown food, two things happen:

- **The Maillard reaction**, which creates savory, roasted flavors out of many amino acid–rich ingredients.

- **Caramelization**, which creates a rich tapestry of flavor depth out of sugars.

If this sounds awfully theoretical to you, think of it this way: browning is the difference between bread and toast, boiled meat and seared steak, and sugar and caramel. In each of these examples, the latter has more complex flavors and more powerful aromas. Simply put: browning makes food delicious.

While instant ramen has a lot of delicious flavors straight out of the packet, it does not include many flavors generated by browning. This is why the Pre-Simmer phase can take your bowl to another level.

SEARING AND SAUTÉING

Searing is the process of cooking ingredients (often meat) at a very high temperature to maximize browning and develop a lot of flavor. It is an excellent technique for browning the exterior of ingredients but it is not ideal for fully cooking them through—due to the high heat, the exterior can burn before the interior fully cooks.

Sautéing is a similar process but is typically done at a medium-high temperature. Ingredients are often moved around the pan to ensure even cooking. It results in some browning but, due to the relatively lower heat, is a better technique for breaking down and fully cooking ingredients.

Between the two, searing is the more useful one for making instant ramen. Since you'll always simmer everything when you cook the noodles, you don't have to worry about fully cooking your ingredients during the Pre-Simmer phase.

Here's how to apply these related techniques when making your instant ramen.

- **Prepare your ingredients.** Make sure your ingredients are not wet. If they are, it will inhibit browning and can cause a lot of messy (and painful) splattering.

- **Heat the saucepan.** Use high heat to sear or medium-high heat to sauté.

- **Add fat, if needed.** Use between 1 teaspoon and 1 tablespoon of fat. If you are cooking meat that is relatively fatty, such as bacon, sausage, SPAM, or ground meat, you don't need to add fat.

- **Cook your ingredients.** If searing, ensure the ingredients are spread out in a thin layer on the saucepan. Let the ingredients cook for a minute without moving them. After that, give the ingredients a turn and sear for another minute or two or until well browned. If sautéing, move ingredients around regularly to ensure even cooking until your desired level of doneness.

- **Scrape up any stuck-on bits.** Once you've added your liquid in the Simmer phase, scrape the bottom of the saucepan to incorporate the flavorful browned bits into your soup. In culinary terms, this is known as *deglazing*.

The above method can be used for your everyday cooking as well. If you're making any kind of stew or saucy dish, try searing or sautéing your ingredients first, before adding any liquids, to enrich your dish with browned flavors.

FLAVOR EXTRACTION

In general, ingredients will impart their flavor onto anything they touch. (Smell your fingers after chopping garlic and this point is clear.) When you simmer ingredients in water, their flavor will go into the water—this is the principle behind making stocks and broths.

However, many flavor-rich compounds dissolve much more easily in fat than in water. As a result, fats are exceptionally good at pulling flavors out of ingredients and then distributing that flavor wherever the fats go. In other words, fats unlock flavor that water cannot.

You can easily test this. In one skillet, try gently cooking garlic in oil for 1 minute. In another skillet, try simmering garlic in water for 1 minute. Taste the garlic oil and compare it to the garlic water. You'll see that the garlic flavor comes through much more strongly in the oil.

So, when you use dry-cooking methods with fats, you bring new levels of flavor out of your ingredients and into your instant ramen.

BLOOMING AND INFUSING

Blooming and infusing are related techniques that involve gently cooking highly aromatic ingredients, such as garlic, ginger, and spices, in fat. These techniques harness the special ability of fat to extract and distribute flavor.

The difference between blooming and infusing is really just a semantic one. We often use the term *blooming* when referring to dry spices, and *infusing* when referring to whole and leafy ingredients such as garlic and herbs. In either case, the principle is the same: add aromatic ingredients to hot oil to extract maximum flavor.

You would be surprised to taste how big of a difference it makes to bloom or infuse your ingredients. The flavors of your aromatics pop. It's like the difference between a black-and-white sketch and a full-color oil painting.

Whenever possible, if you are planning to add an aromatic ingredient to your ramen, I recommend taking advantage of the Pre-Simmer stage to bloom or infuse. If you *also* want to sear or sauté your ingredients during this phase, start with those higher-heat methods first, then lower the heat to move on to blooming or infusing.

> **INGREDIENTS THAT ARE GOOD FOR BLOOMING AND INFUSING**
>
> Berbere, black pepper, coriander, cumin, curry powder, fennel seed, garam masala, garlic, ginger, paprika, red pepper flakes, Sichuan peppercorns, thyme

Here's how to do it:

- **Prepare your ingredients.** If you're using spices, you can use them whole for a milder flavor or ground for a more intense flavor. Whole ingredients such as garlic or ginger should be sliced or minced to increase flavor extraction. Make sure everything is dry to minimize splatter.

- **Heat some fat in a saucepan over medium heat.** If you've already seared or sautéed and there is still some unabsorbed fat in the saucepan, then you're already good to go. Otherwise, add at least another teaspoon of fat.

- **Gently cook the ingredients.** Your goal here is to bring the flavors of the ingredients into the fat. Fifteen seconds to 1 minute is usually enough time—you'll know when your nose picks up the flavors coming out. Ground spices take much less time than whole spices. Keep an eye on your heat and stir regularly to avoid burning the ingredients.

Once you've done all your searing, sautéing, blooming, and infusing, it's time to add your liquids and move on to the next phase.

③ Simmer

The Simmer phase begins once you've brought your liquids to a simmer in your saucepan. This is the main act, when your ramen comes together into a delicious meal.

During this phase, you have two goals:

1 Cook your noodles to achieve a pleasant, chewy texture.

2 Cook your ingredients, improving their flavor and texture, incorporating their flavors into your soup, and, in the case of meat, making them safe to eat.

We may take simmering for granted because it's such a basic technique. However, it's an incredibly important one. First, by fully immersing ingredients in hot water, it cooks them evenly from all directions at once. By contrast, dry-cooking methods are uneven, mostly cooking the parts of ingredients that are in contact with the pan. Second, simmering plays an important function by hydrating starchy ingredients such as noodles, giving them plumpness and body.

Simmering and boiling aren't the same thing, by the way. Simmering means the water is gently bubbling in a way that doesn't violently agitate the ingredients in the saucepan. Boiling, on the other hand, means the water is vigorously bubbling in a way that causes everything in the saucepan to bounce around. For most cooking, this is not desirable, as it can overly jostle your ingredients and also cause excessive evaporation. Adjust the heat as needed to maintain a simmer.

NOODLE COOK TIMES

Once you drop in the noodle cake, the noodles will start hydrating, expanding, and softening at a rapid pace. Because of the way the noodles have been precooked, they'll go from crunchy to chewy to mushy in just a matter of minutes. This is the "instant" part of instant ramen!

If you're not careful, your ramen noodles can become softer than you'd like. It's important to keep an eye on the clock and remember this golden rule:

When the noodles are done, cooking is done.

Don't forget this! This means you need to plan your cooking around the noodles. If you have an ingredient that needs to be cooked for longer than your noodle cook time, it needs to go into the saucepan *before* the noodles.

What is the best level of noodle doneness? That depends on your personal preference. Many people like their noodles to have a good amount of chew—the "al dente" texture that is prized for Italian pasta dishes. Different noodle gauges will require different cook times to become al dente, with thinner noodles generally requiring less time than thicker ones. One thing you should *not* do is trust the directions on the instant ramen packaging. For some reason, they all recommend cooking noodles to a point at which I find them too soft.

If you're not sure what you like, try cooking a noodle cake and pull out some noodles every 30 seconds. Taste them all side by side and see which texture is the most pleasant for you.

However, note that once you've identified your perfect cook time, this is not actually how long you should cook your noodles. That's because once you turn off the heat and put your ramen into a bowl, cooking doesn't end there. Sitting in the hot soup in your bowl, the noodles continue to soften, albeit at a much slower pace.

I recommend a noodle cook time that is at least 30 seconds shorter than your ideal doneness. This provides a buffer for the time it takes to finish and serve your ramen, and then take your first bite.

All of this assumes you're cooking your noodles in a soup made of water and the seasoning sachet. However, you may want to cook your noodles in other liquids, such as milk or gravy. Thicker liquids cook ingredients more slowly, especially if they are acidic, like crushed tomatoes, so you'll need to increase your

NOODLE COOK TIMES AND TEXTURE

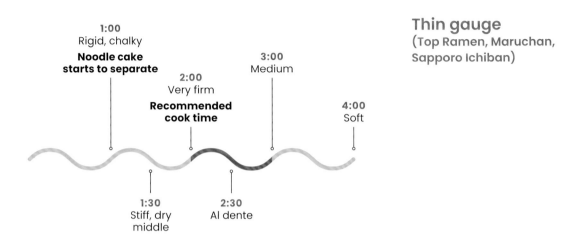

Thin gauge
(Top Ramen, Maruchan, Sapporo Ichiban)

1:00
Rigid, chalky
Noodle cake starts to separate

2:00
Very firm
Recommended cook time

3:00
Medium

4:00
Soft

1:30
Stiff, dry middle

2:30
Al dente

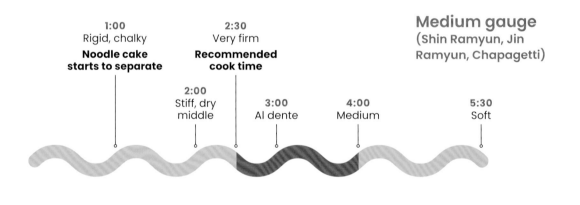

Medium gauge
(Shin Ramyun, Jin Ramyun, Chapagetti)

1:00
Rigid, chalky
Noodle cake starts to separate

2:30
Very firm
Recommended cook time

2:00
Stiff, dry middle

3:00
Al dente

4:00
Medium

5:30
Soft

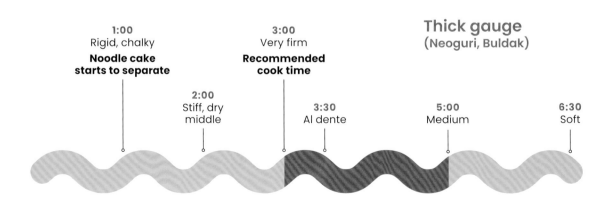

Thick gauge
(Neoguri, Buldak)

1:00
Rigid, chalky
Noodle cake starts to separate

3:00
Very firm
Recommended cook time

2:00
Stiff, dry middle

3:30
Al dente

5:00
Medium

6:30
Soft

cook time. I account for this in the recipes you'll find in this book, and I encourage you to experiment with cook times to find what works best for you.

COOKING LIQUIDS

Instant ramen is unusual in the sense that the noodles are cooked *in* the sauce or soup with which they are served. By contrast, most other noodles, such as Italian pasta, are cooked separately in water and then brought together with their sauce or soup afterward. This means the precise volume of water used to cook pasta is much less of a concern.

With instant ramen, it's important to pay attention to the volume of liquid used to cook your noodles. More liquid means more soup, and that means less concentrated flavors and saltiness and vice versa.

Typically, a packet of instant ramen will instruct you to cook your noodles in 2 cups [475 ml] of water. As you simmer your ramen, some of this water evaporates as steam and some gets absorbed in the noodles. By the time your noodles are cooked, you'll have 1¼ to 1½ cups [300 to 360 ml] of soup left.

This results in a well-portioned bowl of soup noodles. As you'll see in the chart on the next page, it's possible to adjust the liquid volume to achieve different levels of sauciness or soupiness. Note that if you want a particularly soupy dish, you'll need to add salt or other salty ingredients such as soy sauce or fish sauce to maintain proper seasoning.

LIQUID VOLUMES

Liquid Volume	End Result
½ to ¾ cup	Dry noodles
1 cup	Wet but not soupy noodles
1½ to 2 cups	Soup noodles
2½ cups or more	Soup with noodles

TO JIGGLE OR NOT TO JIGGLE

At about the 1-minute mark, most noodle cakes will soften enough to be separated. At this point, you can choose to either leave the noodle cake intact or jiggle and move the noodles around to distribute them throughout the saucepan. If you distribute the noodles, they'll cook a bit faster and, of course, will be more evenly spread out through your bowl. However, you may prefer the aesthetics of having the intact geometric shape of the noodle cake in your bowl. Some dishes, such as Budae Jjigae (page 204), are customarily made with the noodle cake intact.

You may find that you cannot fully immerse your noodle cake in the simmering soup, either because you added a lot of ingredients or decreased the amount of liquid. In this case, you have to actively jiggle and break apart the noodle cake to get it to evenly hydrate and cook. I find it helpful to flip the noodle cake to ensure both sides hydrate enough so it can be broken up. You also need to increase the noodle cook time by at least 30 seconds to account for the initial partial immersion.

SIMMERING INGREDIENTS

In addition to your noodles, you will likely have other ingredients you'd like to add to your dish. You may have already seared or sautéed them during the Pre-Simmer phase. Anything else that needs to be cooked will go in during this Simmer phase.

There are three aspects you'll need to consider when simmering them: **1** quantity, **2** size, and **3** cook time.

Ingredient Quantities

Pay attention to the quantity of ingredients you add to your instant ramen. There is a point at which you've added too much and your noodles won't have enough space to cook properly. Additionally, as described in more detail on page 46, as you add more ingredients, you will need to add salt to maintain adequate seasoning.

A good default rule is this: your total quantity of ingredients can, at most, equal the amount of soup liquid used.

That's to say, if you have 2 cups of liquid, you can add a maximum of 2 cups of ingredients during the Pre-Simmer and Simmer phases. At this maximum level, your saucepan will be a bit crowded but there will still be enough room for your noodle cake to cook, as long as you actively break up and distribute the noodles.

Note that this rule does not apply to ingredients you add at the Finish phase—there are no limits to these toppings.

Ingredient Size

It may seem obvious but it's worth stating: the smaller an ingredient is, the faster it cooks. Conversely, large chunks take a longer amount of time to cook.

Large chunks of meat or vegetables are great for stews and sauces that can simmer all afternoon. However, we're dealing with instant ramen here, and we're optimizing for speed. As a result, remember this rule when it comes to ingredient size for instant ramen: no large chunks.

There are some exceptions if an ingredient is thin enough. One example is a thin, whole fish fillet, which can cook in just a few minutes, even when added frozen (for an example, see the recipe for Moqueca Ramen on page 184). For everything else, you can find a chart of the typical cuts you'll use for instant ramen on page 49. In general, I recommend a maximum width of ½ inch [13 mm] for most vegetables and ¾ inch [2 cm] for meats.

Ingredient Cook Times

Various factors affect how long it takes to cook an ingredient. In general, the more dense and tough or fibrous an ingredient is, the longer it'll take to cook. The definition of "cooked" also depends on your personal taste. Some people may enjoy a slight bite to their green beans while others may prefer soft green beans. There's no right answer—only trying things until you figure out what you like.

For the purposes of making your instant ramen, you don't have to worry too much about overcooking anything because the overall cook times are short. You *do* have to take care to cook things long enough so they're not undercooked.

In terms of timing, there are two approaches to adding your ingredients. You can stagger when you add them by, for example, adding potatoes first, then later adding spinach. This does take more work and attention to the clock. Alternatively, you can simply add everything all at once and let them simmer as long as it takes to cook the slowest cooking ingredient. For example, you could add potatoes and spinach together and let them simmer as long as is needed to cook the potatoes to your desired doneness. This is easier but does mean your spinach may become duller and softer than you'd like.

While there's plenty of room for flexibility for vegetable doneness, it is essential to fully cook raw meats. If you're using ground meat, you have nothing to worry about—the small size of the meat pieces ensures they'll be fully cooked even with the briefest cook time. However, if you're adding chunks of meat, whole shrimp, or pieces of fish, be sure to check that they've cooked through.

VEGETABLE COOK TIMES

Vegetable (thinly sliced)	2:00	3:00	4:00	5:00	6:00
Bell pepper	Crisp-tender	Crisp-tender	Crisp-tender	Tender	Tender
Broccoli	Crunchy	Firm	Crisp-tender	Tender	Tender
Cabbage	Crunchy	Firm	Firm	Firm	Crisp-tender
Carrot	Crunchy	Firm	Crisp-tender	Crisp-tender	Tender
Celery	Crunchy	Crunchy	Crisp-tender	Crisp-tender	Tender
Eggplant	Chewy	Chewy	Chewy	Tender	Tender
Kale	Firm	Firm	Firm	Tender	Tender
Mushroom	Tender	Tender	Tender	Tender	Tender
Peas (fresh)	Crunchy	Firm	Crisp-tender	Crisp-tender	Tender
Potato	Crunchy	Firm	Crisp-tender	Tender	Tender
Zucchini	Crisp-tender	Tender	Tender	Tender	Soft

PROTEIN COOK TIMES

Meat	Recommended Minimum Simmer Time
Bacon	0:30
Beef, ¾ in [2 cm] chunks	3:00 for medium-rare, 4:00 for well-done
Chicken thigh or breast, ¾ in [2 cm] chunks	2:30
Fish, ½ in [13 mm] thick whole fillet, frozen	3:00
Ground meat	0:30
Pork loin, ¾ in [2 cm] chunks	4:00
Shrimp, size 21/25, frozen	4:00
Shrimp, size 31/40, frozen	2:30

For some preparations, you may want to drain your noodles and cooked ingredients at the end of the Simmer phase. You can do this in two ways: either by using the saucepan lid to hold the ingredients back while you pour out the cooking liquid, or by using tongs, a spider skimmer, or a slotted spoon to lift the ingredients out of the cooking liquid.

Note that the cooking liquid does absorb flavor and nutrients, which you'll lose by pouring it out. However, it does open the door to creating saucy dishes (such as Mac 'n' Cheese Ramen, page 224) and dry, dressed noodle dishes (such as Bibim Guksu Ramen, page 231). If you're planning to drain, it's best to reserve the seasoning sachet and add after draining. Without any soup liquid, things can get salty quickly, so you'll typically want to decrease the amount of seasoning—half of the sachet is a good starting point.

④ Finish

The Finish phase begins as soon as you take your saucepan off the heat. You're now just a few steps away from digging into your creation.

During this phase, you have two goals:

❶ Add fresh, prepared, and/or textural toppings to your ramen.

❷ Plate your ramen in an aesthetically pleasing way.

TOPPINGS

There are several reasons why you may want to reserve some ingredients for the Finish phase. One reason is to preserve flavor. Some ingredients, such as basil and other leafy herbs, become dull and shed their flavor quickly if they're cooked. This *can* actually be desirable because the flavor is distributed into the soup. However, sometimes you don't want an ingredient's flavor to be everywhere in your dish and it's preferable to have occasional pops of its flavor. In this case, it's best to add them, fresh, at the end.

Another reason is to preserve texture. When you're adding something to bring crispy, brittle, or dry textural contrast to your ramen, you'll want to add it at the end to minimize the amount of moisture it absorbs from the soup. A good example of this is a nori sheet, which quickly crumples up and loses its structure once it's in contact with a liquid.

The last reason is to improve the appearance of your bowl. If you drizzle chili oil on at the very end, rather than mixing it in during the Simmer phase, you not only preserve the flavor of the oil but also add the visual interest of having streaks of red oil dappling your ramen.

The Finish phase is a great opportunity to build flavor while also making your dish look beautiful. Here are some ideas to try:

Produce

- Scallions
- Basil
- Cilantro
- Parsley
- Bean sprouts
- Cucumber
- Radish
- Tomato
- Peppers
- Avocado
- Corn
- Lemon or lime wedges

Fats and Condiments

- Chili oil (rayu)
- Sesame oil
- Butter
- American cheese
- Cream
- Coconut cream
- Sour cream
- Hot sauce
- Vinegar
- Ketchup

Sprinkles

- Sesame seeds
- Crushed peanuts
- Crumbled potato or tortilla chips
- Bacon bits
- Furikake
- Black pepper
- Chile powder
- Parmesan cheese

Prepared Ingredients

- Leftovers
- Chashu
- Menma (seasoned bamboo shoots, see page 158)
- Ajitsuke Tamago (Jammy Egg, see page 160)
- Nori
- Cold cut meat
- Rotisserie chicken
- Canned fish
- Pickles
- Kimchi

PLATING

Plating is the very last step, when you arrange your creation to be its most beautiful and appetizing self. Don't sleep on this part of the cooking process. Aesthetics are not just about getting a perfect photo for social media. Research has actually verified that we "eat with our eyes," which is to say, appearances affect our perception of flavor. There is no hard science to plating. It depends on your own aesthetic sense. Try using the plating template on page 54 as a starting point. Here are some other things to consider:

- **Use a beautiful bowl.** This is perhaps the easiest way to consistently improve the look of your creations. Most Asian markets, especially Japanese ones, sell bowls that look like the ones used in this book's photography. If you want to shop online, you can look for "45-ounce [1.2 L] ramen bowl," which is the standard size used in Japan.

- **Pay attention to color.** Dishes with multiple vibrant colors tend to look more appetizing than dishes that only have one dull color. If you find that your ramen is looking monochromatic, think about adding a topping that brings a nice colorful contrast. Herbs and scallions are always good options to bring some bright green.

- **Redistribute ingredients added during the Pre-Simmer and Simmer phases.** Once you've poured the ramen into your bowl, take a moment to move the ingredients around to your liking. If you added shrimp, for example, you'll want to make sure they aren't hidden under the noodles.

- **Consider the order in which you add toppings.** You generally want to go from wet to dry. Reserve oils, sprinkles, powders, and time-sensitive ingredients such as nori for the end, in that order. So, for example, you would put down chashu bacon first, then chili oil, then sesame seeds, then smoked paprika, and then nori last.

Now: eat!

PLATING TEMPLATE

Put anything that sticks out between 10 o'clock and 2 o'clock.

Put oils and powders second to last, then finish with anything sensitive to heat or moisture, such as cheese, fresh herbs, and seaweed.

Balance placement so the bowl feels evenly weighted.

Meat is often plated on the side or bottom.

Scallions and fresh herbs can go in the middle or be evenly distributed.

Layer and fan out any sliced items.

Bringing It
All Together

At first, it might take you a little while to execute a bowl of
instant ramen using this method. You might spend a lot
of time pondering ideas, prepping ingredients, and timing
everything just right.

As you become more experienced in this method, the four
steps—Prep, Pre-Simmer, Simmer, Finish—will become familiar
and seamless. I timed myself making recipes from this book
so you can get a sense for what the flow looks like.

SAMPLE TIMELINE FOR TANTANMEN

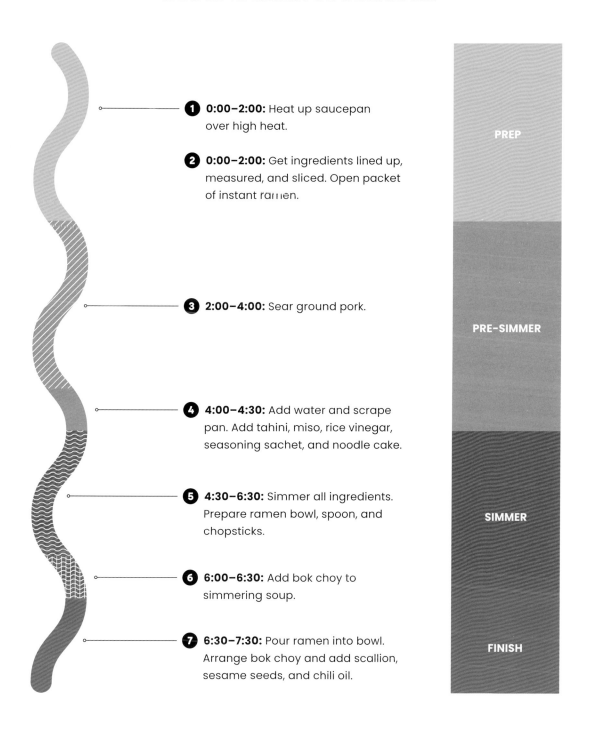

PREP

1 **0:00–2:00:** Heat up saucepan over high heat.

2 **0:00–2:00:** Get ingredients lined up, measured, and sliced. Open packet of instant ramen.

PRE-SIMMER

3 **2:00–4:00:** Sear ground pork.

4 **4:00–4:30:** Add water and scrape pan. Add tahini, miso, rice vinegar, seasoning sachet, and noodle cake.

SIMMER

5 **4:30–6:30:** Simmer all ingredients. Prepare ramen bowl, spoon, and chopsticks.

6 **6:00–6:30:** Add bok choy to simmering soup.

FINISH

7 **6:30–7:30:** Pour ramen into bowl. Arrange bok choy and add scallion, sesame seeds, and chili oil.

Field Guide to
Instant Ramen

Classics

I call these the classics: the low-cost, familiar ones that can be found in every grocery in pretty much every town. These are the ones that, while widely popular, are sometimes dismissively considered "dorm food" or "stoner food." However, this does them a grave disservice.

The classics' simple flavor profiles make them an excellent foundation for creating diverse recipes. Their seasoning sachets, flavorwise, are similar to powdered bouillon. They create straightforward broth-like soups that don't have a prominent Asian flavor profile to them. This allows them to fit in many cuisines, given the near-universal use of chicken, beef, or shrimp broth around the world. As a vegetarian option, soy-flavored soup also melds with many flavors without overpowering them.

For this reason, you'll note that most of my recipe templates use classics. These are the real workhorses of the instant ramen kitchen.

Top Ramen

Top Ramen is produced by Nissin Foods (U.S.A.) Co., Inc. from Nissin Food Products, the longest-standing producer of instant ramen in the world. Their soups tend to focus on primary flavors with neutral-tasting noodles. Top Ramen's soy sauce flavor is one of the few commonly available vegetarian options.

Manufacturer: Nissin Foods (U.S.A.) Co., Inc.

Noodles: Thin with a clean finish

Flavors
- **Soy:** Soy with notes of onion and garlic
- **Chicken:** Chicken with notes of leek
- **Beef:** Beef with notes of ginger
- **Shrimp:** Balanced shrimp with notes of garlic

Maruchan

Maruchan has stronger secondary flavor notes with a touch of nuttiness in the noodles. This brand also boasts the widest range of flavors as well, with varieties such as lime chili shrimp and creamy chicken.

Manufacturer: Maruchan

Noodles: Thin with a slightly nutty finish

Flavors

- **Soy:** Soy and ginger with notes of beef and garlic
- **Chicken:** Chicken, onion, and celery seed
- **Beef:** Beef and soy with notes of leek
- **Shrimp:** Soy and shrimp with notes of leek and celery seed

Sapporo Ichiban

Sapporo Ichiban has springier noodles due to the addition of tapioca starch and its soup flavors are more complex and peppery. The portion size is 15 percent bigger than what you get from Top Ramen or Maruchan.

Manufacturer: Sanyo Foods

Noodles: Thin and springy with soy notes

Flavors

- **Original:** Soy and chicken with notes of onion, sesame, and black pepper
- **Chicken:** Chicken and leek with notes of black pepper; lightly sweet
- **Beef:** Deep beef and soy with notes of black pepper, leek, and garlic
- **Shrimp:** Prominent shrimp with notes of chicken, soy, ginger; lightly sweet

Korean Style

Korean-style instant ramen brands tend to have more complex flavors than the classics. They typically feature thicker, chewier noodles and fiery-red soups that have strong onion and garlic notes. Note that "ramen" in Korean is *ramyeon* or *ramyun*, which is why you'll see it written that way on the packaging.

Their distinctiveness makes them less versatile for creating non-Asian dishes. Don't count them out, though. They are fantastic canvases for improvisation with ingredients, and many of my recipes would work well with Korean-style ones—just be sure to increase the cook time for the noodles accordingly.

If you're just getting started with Korean-style instant ramen, start with Shin Ramyun. It was one of the first instant ramens of this style and is widely enjoyed in Korea.

Shin Ramyun

Beloved by instant ramen eaters around the world, Shin Ramyun is, perhaps, the gold standard for Korean-style instant ramen. I personally grew up eating a lot of it, to such a degree that when I'm sick, I will sometimes "visit Dr. Shin" by whipping one up. The spicy, beefy soup brings me immense comfort (and it does wonders for clearing a stuffy nose!).

Manufacturer: Nongshim

Noodles: Medium with a potato note

Flavors: Fiery beef and black pepper with notes of garlic and onion

Shin Black

In 2011, Nongshim shocked instant ramen lovers by releasing Shin Black, a premium version of Shin Ramyun. It has the same noodles as normal Shin, but the sachets are quite different. It isn't necessarily an improvement over the original Shin, but it does have a different flavor profile.

Manufacturer: Nongshim

Noodles: Medium with a potato note

Flavors: Fiery beef, onion, and garlic with a lightly creamy body and notes of black pepper and mushroom

Jin Spicy

Though lesser known in the United States than its rival Shin Ramyun, Jin Spicy has plenty of devoted fans. Notably, it has a soy- and mushroom-forward flavor instead of Shin's beef-focused soup. (I've seen Jin described as having a "beef bone" flavor, but I don't detect it myself.) It also has a noticeable sweetness to it that helps balance out the fiery, salty, and savory flavors.

Manufacturer: Ottogi

Noodles: Medium with a clean finish

Flavors: Fiery soy sauce and mushroom with light sweetness and notes of garlic

Jin Mild

If you love the flavor of Korean-style instant ramens but their fieriness doesn't love you back, Jin Mild is an excellent option. It has all the flavors and the same chewy noodles as Jin Spicy, but without the fieriness.

Manufacturer: Ottogi

Noodles: Medium with a clean finish

Flavors: Soy sauce and mushroom with light sweetness and notes of garlic

Neoguri

Neoguri distinguishes itself from the pack with its thick, white, chewy noodles and seafood-forward flavor. Its dried vegetable sachet includes bits of seaweed that plump up in the soup, further reinforcing the oceanic theme. It's not just for seafood ingredients, though. It embraces meat just as well as the other brands—as well as pretty much anything else you throw at it.

Manufacturer: Nongshim

Noodles: Thick with a potato note

Flavors: Fiery shellfish, anchovy, and seaweed with notes of black pepper and garlic

Saucy Korean Style

These instant ramen packets create noodles in sauce, rather than soup. They are also tailored to recreating specific Korean noodle dishes, which makes them among the least versatile of the brands. Nonetheless, there's plenty of room to improvise. They both accept proteins, vegetables, and garnishes well. And there are many possibilities for building on the sauces: test out different ways to add aromatics, richness, and brightness, and you may discover some surprisingly delicious results.

Chapagetti

This instant ramen is based on jjajangmyeon, a popular Korean adaptation of a Chinese dish that features chunjang, a fermented black soybean paste. Its noodles are nearly identical to the ones used in Shin Ramyun. It creates a lovely, nutty dark sauce that is bolstered by a sachet of seasoned oil that helps give it some richness.

Manufacturer: Nongshim

Noodles: Medium with a potato note

Flavors: Nutty, roasted soybean paste with light sweetness

Buldak

Buldak is inspired by a Korean dish of the same name, which features barbecued chicken covered in a fiery red sauce. Its noodles are the chewiest of the bunch, retaining their texture even after prolonged simmering. It's also known as being one of the fieriest of the Korean-style instant ramens. You can find varieties of Buldak that claim to have double or even triple the heat of the original.

Manufacturer: Samyang

Noodles: Thick, very chewy, with a clean finish

Flavors: Fiery chicken with light sweetness and notes of soy sauce and onion

Others

The world of instant ramen varieties is boundless. Walk into an Asian supermarket and you'll find an entire section filled with numerous brands, each one touting its unique flavors. In upscale supermarkets and online, you'll find others that claim to be more healthful, more delicious because they're "chef-made," or made with premium ingredients. Taking a step back, there are all the instant ramens that are produced outside the United States too—every country has its own brands. On top of that, the instant ramen landscape is constantly changing. Every season, instant ramen brands come and go.

Given the sheer variety and constant change, it'd be impossible to write up a guide to using each kind of instant ramen. Instead, I focused this field guide on a handful of brands that are commonly available in mainstream supermarkets and have stood the test of time by being on the market for at least a decade.

However, I encourage you to explore the many options out there. It's a lot of fun to grab new varieties and taste your way through them. Importantly, all the techniques and recipes in this book can be used with any brand. Each variety of instant ramen might present a different canvas, but you'll always have your paintbrush to create whatever flavor picture you'd like.

Instant
Flavor Bank

Ramen Flavor Wheel

What makes something delicious? For the most part, it's purely subjective—there is no universal standard for deliciousness. Don't listen to your snobby food friend who claims to know what *truly* makes food tasty. Science is not on their side.

What one person finds appetizing is linked to a number of factors, including their genetics, their cultural background, and their life experiences. Kimchi might be mouthwateringly delicious to a Korean person but repulsive to a French person. A wedge of stinky Camembert cheese might be heaven for a French person but hell for a Korean person.

This basic fact should be liberating. When you're concocting your own recipes for instant ramen, don't worry about what other people might think about it. Think about how it feels for you. If you love ketchup, who cares if some highbrow foodie would scoff at adding it to your ramen? Just do it. If it's tasty, keep it up! If it doesn't seem right, make some adjustments. Be free and be you.

Whatever your taste, it is helpful to think of flavor as a system. It'll help you understand your preferences and build the flavor profile of your recipes. There is no one right way to think of it, but I created the flavor wheel you see on page 69 to help you navigate your way through the possibilities.

Flavor wheels are commonly used in the culinary industry to help understand and describe the flavors of things like wine, coffee, and chocolate. This flavor wheel is different. I created it to guide cooking, not tasting. Pick a flavor dimension that you want to bring to your dish, and the wheel will offer suggested ingredients to take it there. Because flavor is inherently multifaceted, you may see some ingredients appear multiple times in the wheel.

It's not absolutely necessary to cover multiple flavor bases in one dish. Take the example of mac 'n' cheese, a timeless dish that only has rich flavors. It's cheesy, creamy, fatty, and starchy, and it's a perfect dish just like that.

That said, it's also reliably true that a dish will become more intriguing if it touches on a wider spectrum of flavors. As a place to start, add ingredients that cover each of the following key flavor categories: vegetal, acidic, umami, rich, and aromatic.

Applying this approach to mac 'n' cheese, you could add broccoli (vegetal), hot sauce (acidic), bacon (meaty), and cilantro (herbal). You've now got a much more complex dish with more kaleidoscopic flavors.

Over time, I hope you will come to see that, with the right proportions and techniques, almost any flavor combination has the potential to work. This is true for instant ramen, and it's also true for cooking in general. It just takes a creative spirit and a willingness to taste and learn.

Using this flavor wheel as an organizing principle, I've gathered a list of ingredients and pantry suggestions to aid in your own ramen creations. The flavor bank, if you will, captures tips, techniques, and recommended substitutions that will help you develop general cooking skills and be a resource for any dish you develop in the kitchen beyond instant ramen. And because individual ingredients have their own flavor complexities, I've also broken down the supporting flavor profiles to help you adjust your dishes and further develop your palate.

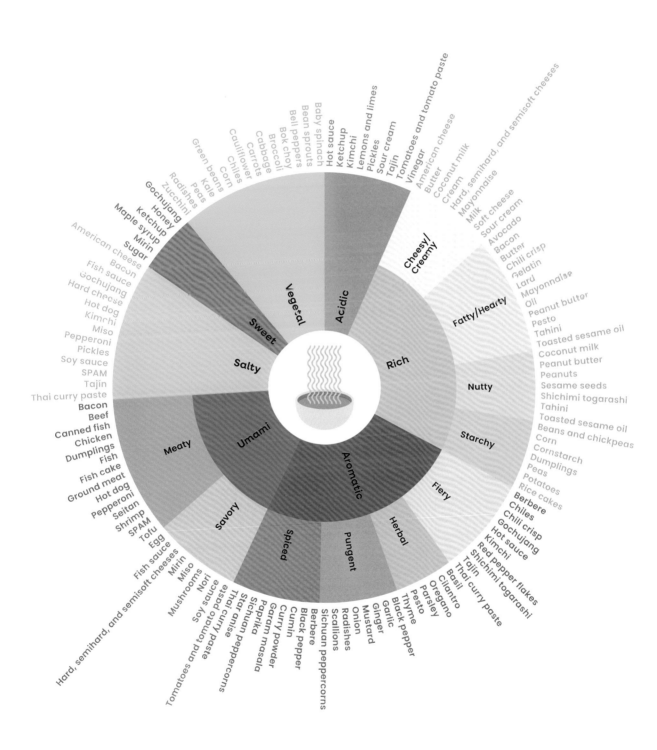

Baby spinach
Bean sprouts
Bell peppers
Bok choy
Broccoli
Cabbage
Carrots
Cauliflower
Chiles
Corn
Green beans
Kale
Peas
Radishes
Zucchini
Gochujang
Honey
Ketchup
Maple syrup
Mirin
Sugar
Bacon
American cheese
Fish sauce
Gochujang
Hard cheese
Hot dog
Kimchi
Miso
Pepperoni
Pickles
Soy sauce
SPAM
Tajín
Thai curry paste
Bacon
Beef
Canned fish
Chicken
Dumplings
Fish
Fish cake
Ground meat
Hot dog
Pepperoni
Seitan
Shrimp
SPAM
Tofu
Egg
Fish sauce
Hard, semihard, and semisoft cheeses
Mirin
Miso
Mushrooms
Nori
Soy sauce
Tomatoes and tomato paste
Thai curry paste
Sichuan peppercorns
Star anise
Sichuan peppercorns
Paprika
Garam masala
Curry powder
Cumin
Black pepper
Berbere
Sichuan peppercorns
Scallions
Radishes
Onion
Mustard
Ginger
Garlic
Black pepper
Thyme
Pesto
Parsley
Oregano
Cilantro
Basil
Tajín
Thai curry paste
Shichimi togarashi
Red pepper flakes
Kimchi
Hot sauce
Gochujang
Chili crisp
Chiles
Berbere
Rice cakes
Potatoes
Peas
Dumplings
Cornstarch
Corn
Beans and chickpeas
Toasted sesame oil
Tahini
Shichimi togarashi
Sesame seeds
Peanuts
Peanut butter
Coconut milk
Toasted sesame oil
Tahini
Pesto
Peanut butter
Oil
Mayonnaise
Lard
Gelatin
Chili crisp
Butter
Bacon
Avocado
Sour cream
Soft cheese
Milk
Mayonnaise
Hard, semihard, and semisoft cheeses
Cream
Coconut milk
Butter
American cheese
Vinegar
Tomatoes and tomato paste
Tajín
Sour cream
Pickles
Lemons and limes
Kimchi
Ketchup
Hot sauce

Cheesy/Creamy
Acidic
Vegetal
Sweet
Salty
Rich
Fatty/Hearty
Nutty
Meaty
Umami
Starchy
Savory
Aromatic
Fiery
Spiced
Pungent
Herbal

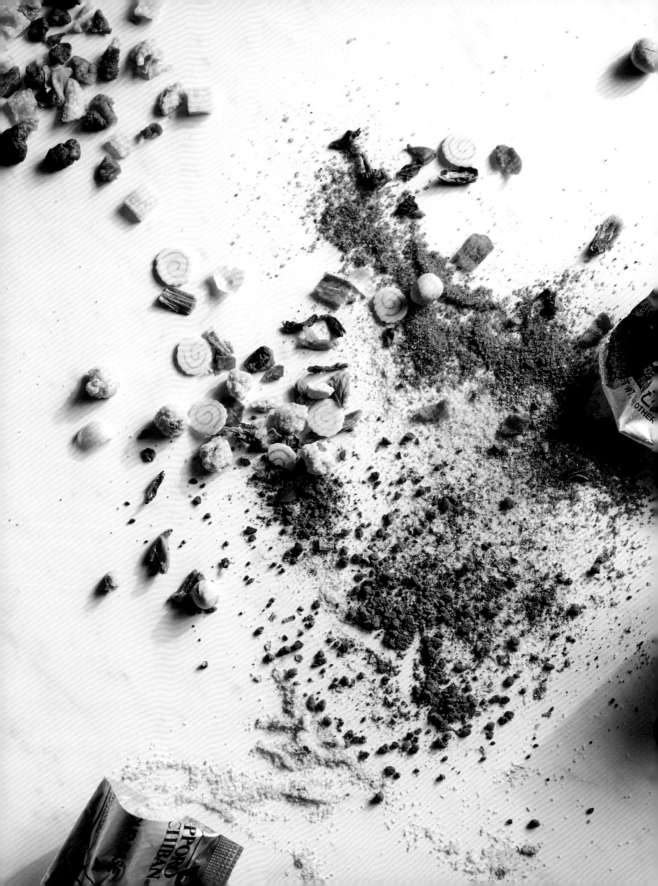

Salty

Ask any chef and they'll probably agree that the single most important flavor note to get right is saltiness—this is referred to as the "seasoning" of a dish. If you do nothing other than season a dish properly, you've done a lot to make it delicious.

Salt is curious because, on its own, it is flavorless and unappetizing. However, in concert with other ingredients, it brings flavors to life, amplifying their distinctiveness and intensity. Without it, food remains bland.

Fortunately, the seasoning sachet that comes with your instant ramen is generally enough to ensure that your final creation is properly salted. The bigger risk, actually, is *overseasoning* your ramen by adding too many salty ingredients. The general rule is this: The more non-salty ingredients you have in your ramen, the more salt you can add.

So, if you add only soy sauce, kimchi, bacon, and gochujang to your instant ramen, all of which are salty, then your final dish risks being unpleasantly salty. Aside from rebalancing the amount of salty and non-salty ingredients, one option is to also decrease the amount of the seasoning sachet that you add.

On the flip side, if you add a lot of non-salty ingredients, you may need to increase your saltiness to maintain appropriate seasoning. That's easy enough to do: add a salty ingredient, or a pinch of salt can always do the trick.

SALINITY CHART

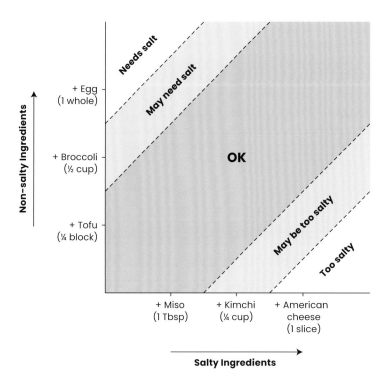

HIT A SALT SNAG?

If you're crying salty tears over an oversalted dish, don't fret, try one of two things:

- Distract from the saltiness by adding other flavors. Acidity, in particular, does wonders for balancing saltiness. Try adding vinegar, citrus, or another acidic ingredient.

- Dilute the saltiness. If you have precooked unsalted ingredients such as rice, potatoes, or vegetables, you can add those. Otherwise, pour out some of the soup and replace it with water or another unsalted liquid.

Sweet

While you may associate sweetness more with dessert, it has an important place in savory dishes as well. In the right dose, it plays a supporting role by amplifying other flavors. As one example, soy sauce on chicken may be tasty, but teriyaki, which is essentially sweetened soy sauce, brings the flavor to a new level of deliciousness. It's no surprise—humans have evolved to like sweetness because it is a sign of calories.

Even where it feels counterintuitive, experiment with adding a bit of sweetness to your savory dishes. While some ingredients are naturally sweet, the easiest way to intentionally add sweetness is to add sugar. Two teaspoons is a good starting point for a dose of sweetness. If you want sweetness and nothing else, granulated sugar is your best bet. Other varieties such as cane sugar or brown sugar work well too. The browner the sugar, the more molasses it likely contains, which brings more distinct flavors that you may or may not want.

You can also try other sources of sweetness, such as honey or maple syrup. They, and other syrups, are typically sweeter than plain sugar by volume, so it's best to decrease the quantity used by at least one-quarter.

Vegetal

This category encompasses the wide world of vegetables, seeds, and nuts that bring both flavor and sustenance to our instant ramen. (Why did I leave out herbs and the onion family? Those vegetables fall under "aromatics" because we tend to add those ingredients more for flavor than sustenance.)

Left to their own devices, most instant ramens don't have any vegetal notes. At best, some have a small sachet of dried vegetables. Even then, it's hardly anything to sink your teeth into and does not meaningfully add any nutritive value. By bringing in vegetal ingredients, you are adding a key new element to your instant ramen.

Vegetal ingredients can bring a wide range of flavors, such as the earthiness of mushrooms, the toastiness of sesame seeds, and the sweetness of carrots. They're an excellent vehicle for adapting your ramen to the season—nothing can beat the flavor of in-season produce.

This category is also the most nutrient-dense, supplying fiber, vitamins, and minerals that are mostly absent in a packet of instant ramen. These ingredients can help you round out the nutritional profile of your instant ramen, making it more of a complete meal.

For most vegetables, if you're cooking them, you have the option of simmering them directly or sautéing them first before simmering them. Sautéing takes a little extra time, but it develops flavors; follow the instructions on page 39 for more.

When you're cutting large vegetables, it's helpful to first slice them into planks, then sticks, and then into dice. Here are the different cuts that are helpful when making instant ramen. There's no need to be fussy about it and cut things perfectly, so consider this just a rough guide.

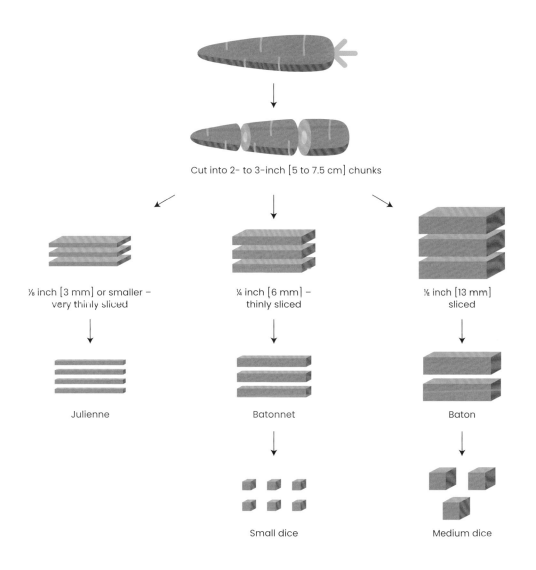

Cut into 2- to 3-inch [5 to 7.5 cm] chunks

⅛ inch [3 mm] or smaller –
very thinly sliced

¼ inch [6 mm] –
thinly sliced

½ inch [13 mm]
sliced

Julienne

Batonnet

Baton

Small dice

Medium dice

When it comes to making instant ramen, frozen vegetables are your friends. They're precut, ready to use, and cook more quickly than fresh vegetables—they were par-cooked before being frozen. If you're using frozen vegetables, they'll take roughly half the time to cook as fresh ones. They can be less flavorful than their fresh counterparts but some do taste surprisingly good, including carrots, broccoli, cauliflower, corn, green beans, kale, and peas.

BABY SPINACH

Spinach is an easy addition to bring leafy, earthy flavors to your ramen, along with a pop of green. Other light leafy greens such as arugula or baby lettuce can be used similarly.

For cooked spinach, add a handful during the Simmer phase and cook for 30 seconds. For a fresh garnish, add raw at the Finish phase.

Flavor profile: Vegetal

BEAN SPROUTS

If you've ever tried chewing on a raw bean, it probably didn't turn out too well for your gut. However, sprouted beans are delicious and bring a pop of freshness. For ramen, the typical sprouts of choice are delicate mung bean and heftier soybean sprouts.

Add ½ to 1 cup [50 to 100 g] during the Simmer phase and cook for 2 minutes for tender sprouts or add a handful, uncooked, at the Finish phase for maximum crunch and freshness.

Flavor profile: Vegetal

BELL PEPPERS

The descendants of chile peppers, bell peppers have been bred to be sweet rather than fiery. Green bell peppers are unripe and have less sweetness and a more grassy flavor than the other colors.

Add a quarter to half of a pepper, thinly sliced, sautéed, or simmered for at least 2 minutes.

Flavor profile: Vegetal

BOK CHOY

A leafy relative of the cabbage, bok choy has a delicately crisp texture when raw or lightly cooked. Be careful about overcooking it, as it can become chewy and stringy.

Chop 2 to 4 leaves and add raw at the Finish phase or add 2 to 4 whole leaves in the last 30 seconds of the Simmer phase.

Flavor profile: Vegetal

BROCCOLI

Broccoli is like a bouquet—each of those little green buds is actually an unopened flower. These buds brown quickly when cooked in oil and develop pleasant nutty flavors.

Add ½ to 1 cup [35 to 70 g] of small florets, sautéed or simmered for at least 3 minutes.

Flavor profile: Vegetal

CABBAGE

Good ol' reliable cabbage: it is nutritious, flavorful, cheap, and long-lasting when refrigerated. It takes a bit more simmering than other vegetables to reach a tender texture. Like broccoli, it browns easily and develops nutty flavors when cooked in oil.

Add ½ to 1 cup [40 to 80 g], diced small, sautéed or simmered for at least 4 minutes.

Flavor profile: Vegetal

CARROTS

Carrots bring gentle, earthy sweetness to any dish. As a relatively dense and crunchy vegetable, large chunks are not suitable for instant ramen, as they take too long to soften. Peeling carrots decreases some of the bitterness but is not absolutely necessary if you're in a hurry.

Add ½ to 1 cup [70 to 140 g], diced small or thinly sliced, sautéed or simmered for at least 4 minutes.

Flavor profile: Vegetal

CAULIFLOWER

Like broccoli, cauliflower is also composed of flower stalks. It is less fibrous than broccoli, which gives it a particularly tender texture when cooked.

Add ½ to 1 cup [70 to 140 g] of small florets, sautéed or simmered for at least 3 minutes.

Flavor profile: Vegetal, starchy

CORN

These golden grains bring juicy sweetness and color as a topping to your ramen. Canned corn is prized by Koreans for its sweetness and tender texture. Fresh corn, raw or briefly cooked, is excellent when in season and will have more vibrant flavors and more texture.

Add ¼ to ½ cup [35 to 70 g] during the Simmer phase and cook for at least 2 minutes if fresh or 30 seconds if canned. You can also add 2 tablespoons, fresh or canned, at the Finish phase.

Flavor profile: Vegetal, starchy

TIP: KOREAN CORN CHEESE TOPPING

Koreans go nuts for "corn cheese," which is a gooey mix of corn and mozzarella. It's a great side dish or can be used as a topping for your ramen too. To make it, in a small skillet, combine one 8.75-ounce [245 g] can of corn, drained, with 2 tablespoons of mayonnaise and ¾ cup [60 g] of shredded mozzarella. Broil for 5 to 7 minutes, or until lightly browned.

GREEN BEANS

These pods have a satisfying multilayered texture, especially when cooked crisp-tender. If you like the texture of long-stewed, pliant green beans, use frozen green beans—fresh ones take a very long time to cook down to that point.

Add ¾ to 1½ cups [105 to 210 g] of cut green beans during the Simmer phase and cook for at least 5 minutes.

Flavor profile: Vegetal

KALE

This leafy member of the cabbage family develops a tender, buttery texture with just a few minutes of cooking. When sautéed, it readily develops roasted flavors. Green curly and lacinato kale are the most common types, but you can use any variety.

Add 1 or 2 leaves, thinly sliced, sautéed or simmered for at least 5 minutes.

Flavor profile: Vegetal

PEAS

These seeds have a more delicate texture and sweeter flavor than their bean cousins. If you can't find fresh ones, frozen peas are an excellent option. While some recipes call for a long simmer, I prefer the pop of a lightly cooked pea.

Add ¼ to ½ cup [35 to 70 g] during the Simmer phase and cook for 30 seconds.

Flavor profile: Vegetal, starchy

RADISHES

These vegetables have a pungent, peppery kick to them and are crisp when fresh and delicate when cooked long enough. The daikon variety is often used in East Asian cuisines and has a milder flavor.

Add ½ to 1 cup [60 to 120 g], diced small, during the Simmer phase and cook for at least 5 minutes. For a fresh garnish, add ¼ cup [30 g], very thinly sliced, at the Finish phase.

Flavor profile: Vegetal, pungent

ZUCCHINI

The beauty of this summer squash is its tender texture and quick cook time. Avoid letting it simmer too long or it will break down entirely. Other summer squash such as pattypan or yellow squash can be used similarly.

Add ½ to 1 cup [70 to 140 g], sliced, at the Simmer phase and cook for at least 2 minutes.

Flavor profile: Vegetal

Acidic

Acidic ingredients are perceived by our tongue as sour. In the context of a dish, these ingredients give us the perception of eating something that is brighter and more vivid.

Consider the difference between two pieces of fish: one with lemon squeezed on it, and one without. The former seems to pop with a flavor that is livelier than the latter. This is the power of acidic ingredients: they cast light on the flavors of a dish while also bringing roundness and balance to other notes, such as bitterness or sweetness. Acidic ingredients also help cut through the heaviness of fatty or rich dishes. Consider, for example, how ketchup balances out deep fried french fries or how pickles help lighten up a fatty cheeseburger.

One easy way to bring some acidic brightness to your dish is to squeeze in some fruit, especially from the citrus family, such as lemons or limes. You'd be surprised by how many different flavor profiles can benefit from a touch of acidity.

CANNED TOMATOES

Canned tomatoes are a blessing—they are picked at peak ripeness and then sealed up, able to be summoned at any time, in any kitchen. While tomatoes lose texture and their flavors dull a bit when they are canned, they keep much of their aroma and savoriness. I find canned crushed or ground tomatoes to be the most useful because they work well to thicken soups.

Replace ½ to 1 cup [120 to 240 ml] of water with canned crushed or ground tomatoes. You may need to increase the cooking time of anything that simmers in the tomatoes, including your noodle cake.

Flavor profile: Acidic, savory

KETCHUP

It may be one of the most common condiments, but ketchup deserves respect as a perfectly balanced combination of savory tomatoes, sweet sugar, and acidic vinegar, along with some aromatics. While we know it mostly as a dip and spread, it works well to enrich a soup with its flavor and a touch of body.

Stir 2 to 4 tablespoons into the soup during the Simmer phase. For a more intense pop of ketchup flavor, squirt ketchup in a pattern over your dish in the Finish phase.

Flavor profile: Acidic, sweet

KIMCHI

If there is one dish that defines Korean cuisine, it's kimchi. There are numerous varieties, but the most common one is made with napa cabbage fermented in a spicy, garlicky seafood brine. If you don't have kimchi, you can substitute sauerkraut with a pinch of red pepper flakes.

Add ¼ to ½ cup [35 to 75 g] during the Simmer phase and cook for at least 2 minutes. For a zesty, fiery topping, add in the Finish phase. You can also add the kimchi pickling liquid to intensify the flavor.

Flavor profile: Acidic, fiery, salty

LEMONS AND LIMES

You may find it odd to squeeze citrus on your ramen, but it really works. The Japanese themselves often add yuzu, a tart citrus fruit, to their ramen. Lemons tend to be associated more with temperate cuisines and limes more with tropical cuisines, but they can be used interchangeably.

Squeeze in the juice of a wedge, up to one-quarter of the fruit, at the Finish phase, taking care not to add any seeds. For more depth and a touch of bitterness, add the zest, which contains oils that have a wider range of flavors.

Flavor profile: Acidic

TIP: ZESTING CITRUS

When zesting a citrus fruit, your goal is to remove just the colorful outer layer, which contains flavorful oils, without digging into the bitter white pith beneath. You can do this with a box grater or a Microplane. If using a box grater, place it on a plate or cutting board and gently run the fruit up and down the grating holes, turning the fruit as you go. If you have a Microplane, zest directly into the saucepan using the same technique.

PICKLES

Pickles are vegetables preserved in brine or vinegar. While the most common American pickle is a cucumber, many vegetables can be pickled. If the vegetable is one that could be cooked normally, you can also cook its pickled version. Whatever your pickle of choice, it can bring welcome brightness to the savory flavors of instant ramen.

To infuse the soup with acidity, add ¼ to ½ cup [35 to 70 g], diced or sliced, during the Simmer phase and cook for at least 2 minutes. For a crisp, acidic topping, add at the Finish phase.

Flavor profile: Acidic, salty

TOMATOES

Fresh tomatoes add pops of tender, juicy savoriness and brightness to your ramen. The best option is an in-season tomato from a farmers' market. The second best option is a pack of cherry or grape tomatoes from the supermarket. Avoid those lifeless, large refrigerated tomatoes at the supermarket. They've lost all flavor and can have a mealy texture.

Add ½ cup [80 g] diced (about 6 cherry tomatoes sliced in half) or more, sautéed or simmered for at least 2 minutes. For a fresh topping, add raw at the Finish phase.

Flavor profile: Acidic, savory

VINEGAR

Vinegar is a magical liquid, the result of using bacteria to convert alcohol to acetic acid, which gives the liquid its distinct tartness. There are countless varieties of vinegar, but my three favorite ones are rice vinegar (for more neutral tartness), apple cider vinegar (for a fruitier touch), and sherry vinegar (for nutty, caramelly notes). All vinegars are a convenient and quick addition to brighten up your ramen.

Add 1 teaspoon or more during the Simmer phase.

Flavor profile: Acidic

Umami

Umami flavors: they're the mouthwatering, delicious notes associated with roasted meat, soy sauce, Parmesan cheese, and tomatoes. Savory foods are rich with the taste of umami, which comes from glutamate, an amino acid and building block of protein. It's a flavor note that plays a central role in every cuisine.

Instant ramen already has certain aspects of savoriness dialed up. The seasoning sachets have ingredients such as MSG, yeast extract, or hydrolyzed protein, all of which are rich with glutamates. It's a big reason why instant ramen is so satisfying to eat. Even so, there's no ceiling to savoriness, and you'll find that adding a dollop of miso or a splash of soy sauce can bring a nice lift to your bowl.

However, as noted on page 38, instant ramen packets generally lack one category of umami flavors: the roasted, caramelly notes generated by browning. You can add this by browning your ingredients or adding ingredients that have already been browned, such as rotisserie chicken.

MSG, short for *monosodium glutamate*, is the sodium salt of glutamic acid, an amino acid that is produced by our bodies and is naturally found in many foods, including seaweed, tomatoes, and cheese. It is one of a group of chemicals that is responsible for the taste sensation of umami, which can also be described as savoriness or meatiness.

In 1968, the *New England Journal of Medicine* published a letter to the editor written by a Chinese American doctor about how he felt ill after eating at Chinese restaurants. He speculated that salt, cooking wine, or MSG might be responsible for this. In the context of prevailing discriminatory attitudes toward the Chinese at the time, news outlets latched onto this and labeled it "Chinese restaurant syndrome," a feeling of sickness caused by the use of MSG. This provoked a nationwide perception of MSG as a toxic ingredient.

However, no scientific studies have shown any link between the consumption of MSG and ill health. Nonetheless, due to the controversy around MSG, you may notice that some instant ramen brands will advertise that their product contains no MSG. Instead, hydrolyzed proteins and autolyzed yeasts are used, which, like MSG, are also sources of glutamic acid.

BACON

Bacon cooks quickly and delivers a lot of fatty, smoky, porky flavor, so it's perfect for instant ramen. It's best to gently warm the bacon rather than sear it over high heat—this helps render out the fat so it can enrich your soup.

Add 1 to 2 ounces [30 to 55 g] (1 or 2 thin-sliced strips), sliced, to a cold saucepan and heat over medium-high heat. Once the bacon starts sizzling and releasing its fat, cook for 2 to 4 minutes, depending on your desired doneness.

Flavor profile: Meaty, fatty/hearty, salty

BEEF

Beef works well as long as you pick the right cut. Skip stew meats such as chuck, which require a long cook time to become tender, and stringy belly cuts such as strip or flank, which become tough when boiled. Instead, use tender cuts of meat that work well on the grill, such as sirloin or strip.

Add 4 ounces [115 g], cut into ¾-inch [2 cm] cubes, during the Simmer phase and cook for at least 3 minutes for medium-rare or, for roasted flavors, sear in at least 1 teaspoon of fat over high heat for 3 minutes or until browned all over.

Flavor profile: Meaty

CANNED FISH

Canned fish fillets can be quite delicious—especially flavorful, savory varieties such as sardines, mackerel, and anchovies. Right out of the can, the fish are fully cooked, tender, and ready to eat, making them an easy addition to your dish.

Add 2½ to 3½ ounces [70 to 100 g] (2 or 3 canned sardines), whole, at the Finish phase. To incorporate the fish into your soup, add at any point during the Simmer phase and allow the fish to break apart. If you're using anchovies, which have a potent flavor, you can use much less.

Flavor profile: Meaty

CHICKEN

Chicken is one of the fastest-cooking whole cuts of meat you can use. While any cut can work, use chicken thighs for best results. If possible, salt the chicken at least an hour in advance to allow the seasoning to penetrate. (Pre-salted meat stays juicier and is more flavorful.)

Add 4 to 6 ounces [115 to 170 g] (about 1 boneless, skinless thigh), cut into ½-inch [13 mm] cubes, during the Simmer phase and cook for at least 3 minutes or, for roasted flavors, sear in at least 1 teaspoon of fat over high heat for 3 minutes or until browned all over.

Flavor profile: Meaty

DUMPLINGS

It's always a good idea to have a bag of dumplings in the freezer. They're a quick and easy addition to instant ramen to bulk it out and add some protein. Be careful, though: many frozen dumplings contain raw meat that you need to cook thoroughly during the Simmer phase. I've included an easy make-at-home recipe for wontons on page 168.

Add 3 or more dumplings, depending on their size, during the Simmer phase and cook according to the recipe or package directions.

Flavor profile: Meaty, starchy

EGG

If there is *one* protein to add to your ramen, it's the egg. It cooks quickly and brings a perfect level of savoriness to the bowl. It's also incredibly versatile, providing different textures and flavors depending on how it's cooked.

Add 1 or 2 eggs and cook in one of the following ways.

- **Jammy:** For a traditional jammy ramen egg, follow the recipe on page 160.

- **Poach:** Crack the egg(s) directly into the simmering soup and let it simmer for 2 to 3 minutes for a runny yolk, 5 minutes for a fully cooked egg. When you add the noodle cake, do your best to not agitate the egg.

- **Scramble:** Beat the egg(s) in a bowl. Heat 1 tablespoon of oil or fat in the saucepan over medium-high heat. Add the eggs and scramble. Once the eggs are set, add water to start the Simmer phase.

- **Swirl:** Beat the egg(s) in a bowl. Give the simmering soup a stir and then pour the eggs in to create egg ribbons. Alternatively, crack the egg(s) directly into the saucepan and stir the eggs in the soup to create egg ribbons. The faster you stir the soup, the finer the ribbons will be. Let simmer for at least 30 seconds.

Flavor profile: Savory

FISH

Two common kinds of fish that work well with instant ramen are salmon and whitefish. Whitefish is an imprecise category, but it covers fish with mild, white, flaky flesh such as tilapia, mahi mahi, and cod. If you can find frozen fillets that are sufficiently thin, you can cook them whole, directly out of the freezer, which is quite convenient. If possible, salt the fish 30 minutes in advance to allow the seasoning to penetrate.

Use a 3- to 5-ounce [85 to 140 g] fillet. If it is thin (about ½ inch [13 mm] thick), you can leave it whole. Otherwise, slice the fillet. Add during the Simmer phase and cook for at least 2 minutes if fresh and 3 minutes if frozen. Check to ensure the fish is fully cooked before serving.

Flavor profile: Meaty

FISH CAKE

Also known as *narutomaki* in Japan, these pink and white disks are made from a cooked fish paste and have a bouncy texture. They're used principally as garnish to add a pop of pink to the bowl.

Add 1 to 3 slices at the Finish phase.

Flavor profile: Meaty

FISH SAUCE

This condiment is made from fermented fish and is one of the most savory, umami-rich ingredients you can find. Don't be too concerned about it bringing a heavy seafood note to your dish. Think of it more like an alternative to soy sauce. While it is indeed made from fish, it's surprisingly complementary to many flavors without adding a particular fishy note.

Add ½ to 1 teaspoon during the Simmer phase.

Flavor profile: Savory, salty

GROUND MEAT

If you want to add meat to your instant ramen, ground meat is the best way to go. It can be seared and fully cooked within a few minutes. Because it is cut so small, it also absorbs the flavors of the soup. I typically use ground beef or pork, but any kind of ground meat works well. Fresh sausage can also be used similarly.

Add 2 to 4 ounces [55 to 115 g] of meat during the Simmer phase and cook for at least 3 minutes or, for roasted flavors, sear over high heat for 3 minutes or until browned all over. Most ground meat is fatty enough to be seared without the addition of oil. However, if it is lean, sear it in 1 teaspoon of fat.

Flavor profile: Meaty

HOT DOG

The humble hot dog is an ideal sausage to add to instant ramen. Each link is one good portion, bringing welcome bursts of salty savoriness with every bite. It's also precooked, so it can be added at any point without any concern about under-cooking. Other precooked sausages such as kielbasa can be used similarly.

Add 2 to 4 ounces [55 to 115 g] (1 or 2 hot dogs), sliced. Add at any point during the Simmer phase or, for roasted flavors, sear the hot dog slices over high heat for 2 minutes or until browned. Hot dogs can usually be seared without the addition of fat.

Flavor profile: Meaty, salty

MIRIN

This rice wine is used in Japanese cuisine to enrich marinades and sauces. For instant ramen, its sweet, savory, and syrupy consistency adds body and complexity to your bowl. It requires some cooking to burn off the alcohol. Note that once the mirin is mixed with water, the alcohol cooks off much more slowly.

Use 2 tablespoons or more at the Pre-Simmer phase and cook for a minute or until the mirin has reduced to a thicker consistency.

Flavor profile: Savory, sweet

MISO

Miso is a soybean paste that has gone through a lengthy fermentation process that produces a delicious range of nutty and savory flavors. It is one of the most versatile condiments, and there is hardly a savory dish that would not welcome a touch of miso.

Add 1 to 2 tablespoons during the Simmer phase before adding the noodle cake. Stir until it has completely dissolved into the soup.

Flavor profile: Savory, salty

TIP: MAGIC MISO MARINADE

Three ingredients—miso, mirin, and sugar—are all you need to create a magically delicious marinade that works on pretty much any protein or vegetable. The recipe is simple and worth memorizing: 1 part miso, 1 part mirin, and ½ part sugar. Mix it together. Salt your ingredients and coat with the marinade for at least 2 hours, up to 2 days. Wipe the marinade off before cooking. Enjoy!

MUSHROOMS

There is a wide universe of flavors to be found in these fungi. All varieties share in common an umami-rich savoriness and a texture that is meaty and slightly spongy. Mushrooms soften quickly but retain their meaty texture even with extended cooking. You can develop delicious flavors by sautéing them, though it takes some time.

Add 4 to 6 button mushrooms (or equivalent if using another kind of mushroom), sliced or halved, during the Simmer phase and cook for at least 2 minutes. For rich, roasted flavors, add mushrooms, dry, to the saucepan. Cook for 6 minutes or until all the liquid has evaporated, then add 1 teaspoon of fat and sauté for 3 more minutes or until the slices are browned.

Flavor profile: Savory

NORI (SEAWEED SHEETS)

Dried seaweed is one of the most umami-rich ingredients in the world. It's considered an essential ramen component that adds savory flavor, as well as both textural and visual contrast to the bowl. The standard size for a sheet is about 8 by 7 inches [20 by 17.5 cm]. While it is traditionally cut into quarters for ramen, I find this size to be a bit unwieldy.

Take a full-size toasted nori sheet and, using a knife, cut it into 6 equal-size rectangles. Alternatively, you can use toasted sea-weed snacks. Add 3 or 4 pieces at the Finish phase just before eating. Contact with the soup will quickly cause the nori to shrivel up.

Flavor profile: Savory

PEPPERONI

This pizza staple is a wonderfully convenient ingredient for cooking with instant ramen. It's presliced, browns beautifully on its own, and adds a nice combination of porky fattiness and spice. Any kind of salami, such as soppressata, can be used similarly.

Use 1 to 2 ounces [30 to 55 g]. Add at any point during the Simmer phase or, for roasted flavors, sear the slices over medium-high heat for 2 minutes or until browned.

Flavor profile: Meaty, salty

SEITAN

Of all the plant-based ground meat substitutes out there, I prefer seitan, a staple in Asian cuisines for many centuries. Made from vital wheat gluten, it has a firm, meaty texture and pleasant, savory flavor. Depending on the preparation, the flavor profile can vary from heavily seasoned to neutral.

Use 2 to 4 ounces [55 to 115 g], crumbled. Add at any point during the Simmer phase or, for roasted flavors, sauté in 1 tablespoon of fat over medium-high heat for 2 minutes or until browned and there are pieces stuck to the saucepan. Scrape up the stuck bits when you add the liquid.

Flavor profile: Meaty

SHRIMP

This crustacean is a convenient protein because it brings gentle seafood flavor to your ramen and cooks well directly from the freezer. While it's convenient that shrimp cooks so quickly, it also means they can quickly go from raw to rubbery and overcooked, so keep a close eye on timing and always check that they are fully cooked before digging in. I recommend using peeled and deveined shrimp to maximize ease of use.

Add 3 to 4½ ounces [85 to 135 g] (6 to 9 shrimp, 31/40 size) during the Simmer phase and cook for 2½ minutes from frozen. If using jumbo shrimp (21/25 size), simmer for 4 minutes. If using thawed shrimp, decrease the cook time by 30 seconds.

Flavor profile: Meaty

SOY SAUCE

A classic ingredient that has been in use for thousands of years, soy sauce is a powerfully flavorful liquid derived from fermented soybeans. Just a little bit can inject an immense amount of savoriness. It is highly salty, though, so you'll need to take care not to overseason your ramen.

Add 1 to 3 teaspoons during the Simmer phase. If you are using more than 1 teaspoon, consider decreasing the amount of the seasoning sachet that you add to avoid overseasoning your dish.

Flavor profile: Savory, salty

SPAM

This canned pork product was a staple part of US military rations during World War II. Over the course of the war, it became a beloved part of many Pacific Ocean food cultures. With its robust pork flavor, fattiness, and tender texture, it's no wonder it caught on.

Add one-quarter to one-third of a 12-ounce [340 g] can, sliced or diced. Add at any point during the Simmer phase or, for roasted flavors, add to a cold saucepan over high heat. Once it starts sizzling, sear for 2 minutes or until browned.

Flavor profile: Meaty, salty

TOFU

On its own, tofu has a mild taste. However, it has a pleasant texture, readily takes on other flavors, and can develop some meaty flavors when browned in oil. Use firm or extra-firm tofu when you want it to remain intact. Use silken tofu when you want it to meld into the soup.

Add a quarter to half of a 14- to 16-ounce [390 to 455 g] block of tofu, cubed. Add at any point during the Simmer phase or, for roasted flavors, sear in at least 1 tablespoon of fat over high heat until browned. This may take a while, so it is not recommended if you are in a hurry.

Flavor profile: Meaty

TOMATO PASTE

This thick paste is made from tomatoes that have been cooked down and concentrated. It packs intense tomato flavor with an umami-rich savoriness. On top of that, it works well as a soup thickener. Because it has such a low moisture content, tomato paste browns well, developing even more complex savory flavors.

Add 1 to 2 tablespoons during the Simmer phase and stir to incorporate into your soup. For caramelly, browned flavors, sauté over medium-high heat in at least 1 teaspoon of fat for 30 seconds or until fragrant but not burned.

Flavor profile: Savory, acidic

Rich

If you've ever eaten traditional Japanese ramen, you may have noticed that the soup typically has a lot of richness to it. This is the result of using stock made from bones simmered over many hours, enriching it with gelatin and giving it a lush texture. Ramen makers also incorporate fat into the soup, further fortifying it. The end result is something that practically coats your mouth with deliciousness.

On this front, instant ramen can't compete. Straight out of the package, its soup may be flavorful, but it is typically quite thin and watery. There's only so much that the seasoning sachet can do. One of the most important things you can do to make your instant ramen more satisfying is to add ingredients that contribute richness to the soup. Ingredients in this category bring heft and body to your bowl.

There are several ways to achieve this. You can add creamy or fatty ingredients to bring some body to the soup, or you can thicken it with a starch. However, one of my favorite ways to enrich the soup is by adding powdered gelatin (see page 102), which gives the soup the feeling of having been made with a long-simmered stock. However you do it, experiment with building body in your soups and you'll have a satisfying bowl every time.

AMERICAN CHEESE

Don't turn your nose up at this processed cheese product. American cheese has the distinctive ability to melt smoothly at a relatively low temperature, and it's an excellent addition to fortify a soup with creamy cheesiness.

Add 1 or 2 slices at the Finish phase. It'll retain its square shape at first but then melt into the soup once you give it a stir.

Flavor profile: Cheesy/creamy, salty

AVOCADO

The avocado is a rare example of a fruit that is rich in fat. Don't cook it, though—it will develop unpleasant, bitter flavors. As a topping, it adds a smooth, buttery note to your ramen. Wrap any leftover avocado tightly with plastic wrap to prevent browning.

Add a quarter to half of an avocado, sliced, at the Finish phase.

Flavor profile: Fatty/hearty

BEANS AND CHICKPEAS (CANNED)

Beans and chickpeas are protein- and fiber-rich legumes with a creamy, starchy texture. They can add heft to your bowl and, if mashed, give your soup a fuller body. They have good flavor and texture in canned form and require no additional cooking.

Use ½ to 1 cup [70 to 140 g], drained. Add with the noodle cake during the Simmer phase or, to thicken the soup, mash ¼ cup [35 g] of the beans in the saucepan during the Pre-Simmer phase, just before adding the liquid.

Flavor profile: Starchy

BUTTER

Is butter the greatest fat of all time? It's certainly a contender in my book. Nothing compares to the ability of butter to bring warm, golden creaminess to a dish, and instant ramen is no exception.

Use 1 to 2 tablespoons. To sear or sauté ingredients, heat it in the saucepan over medium to medium-high heat during the

Pre-Simmer phase. If the butter starts to brown (without burning), it will take on a pleasant nutty flavor. For maximum butter flavor, top your ramen with it at the Finish phase. It will gradually melt and infuse its flavor into the soup.

Flavor profile: Cheesy/creamy, fatty/hearty

COCONUT MILK

Thanks to its high saturated fat content, this creamy liquid works well as a vegan option to bring body and richness to your soup. It's also worth stocking coconut milk powder, which is available online. It's a useful shelf-stable ingredient, and it reconstitutes well, making it a delicious and convenient ingredient for instant ramen.

Replace ½ to ¾ cup [120 to 180 ml] of water with coconut milk.

Flavor profile: Cheesy/creamy, nutty

CORNSTARCH

Cornstarch is highly effective at thickening your soup and even turning it into a sauce. Don't add it directly to your simmering soup, though, as it will clump up instead of dissolving.

Use 1 tablespoon to thicken your soup, 2 tablespoons to create a gravy-like consistency. Reserve ¼ cup [60 ml] of water, keeping it at room temperature, and mix the cornstarch with the water to make a smooth white slurry, then add it to your ramen with 1 minute left in the Simmer phase.

Flavor profile: Starchy

CREAM

Cream has a more pronounced dairy flavor than milk, and only a small amount is needed to add fattiness and creaminess to your soup.

Add 1 to 4 tablespoons during the Simmer phase. If you're using more than ¼ cup [60 ml], decrease the amount of water by an equivalent amount. For an appealing presentation, drizzle the cream around the soup at the Finish phase.

Flavor: Cheesy/creamy

GELATIN (POWDERED)

Gelatin is a protein derived from collagen, which is a connective tissue found in abundance in animal bones. Cooks typically simmer bones for hours to extract gelatin, which gives the soup a luscious, rich mouthfeel. This is one of the secrets to the richness of traditional Japanese ramen: the soup is extremely rich in gelatin.

Fortunately, you can buy gelatin in powder form at the supermarket and achieve a similar result instantly—no long simmer needed. I consider it an essential ingredient for cooking with instant ramen. You can substitute 3 sheets of leaf gelatin for one ¼-ounce [7 g] sachet of powdered gelatin. As a vegan option, you can achieve a similar effect by substituting 2 teaspoons of agar agar for 1 sachet of gelatin.

Use 1 or 2 sachets (1 to 2 tablespoons). Powdered gelatin must be hydrated before being heated. Add it to the water or liquid you will use at room temperature and give it a vigorous stir. Let it hydrate for at least 1 minute and then stir it again before heating.

Be careful: water with gelatin in it can foam as it heats up. Lower the heat or give it a stir to decrease foaming. The foaming will subside once you add ingredients.

Flavor profile: Fatty/hearty

HARD CHEESE

Hard cheeses such as Parmesan, Pecorino Romano, and grana padano have been pressed and, in many cases, aged to develop potent savory flavors. Because of their firm texture, they are typically grated into dishes. If you are interested in adding umami-rich cheesy flavor to your dish, they are your best bet.

Add 1 to 4 tablespoons toward the end of the Simmer phase and stir to incorporate into your soup. To use as a garnish, add at the Finish phase.

Flavor profile: Cheesy/creamy, savory, salty

LARD

Animal fat is one of the best ingredients for bringing succulent, rich fattiness to your soup. The Japanese certainly know this and often incorporate large amounts of lard into their ramen. Lard is commonly available in US supermarkets, and bacon fat is a good option as well. The next time you make bacon, save the fat in a jar for up to three months.

Use 1 to 2 tablespoons. To sear or sauté ingredients, heat it in the saucepan over medium to medium-high heat during the Pre-Simmer phase. Otherwise, add the fat at the beginning of the Simmer phase—the simmering action will help incorporate the fat into your soup.

Flavor profile: Fatty/hearty

MAYONNAISE

Mayonnaise demonstrates the extraordinary potential of ingredients to transform when combined. Oil and eggs—normally liquid on their own—combine to make a spreadable, opaque, creamy condiment. For ramen, it works well to enrich your soup. Don't let it simmer, though, because it'll break and lose some of its textural powers.

Add 1 to 2 tablespoons at the Finish phase and mix into the soup. To allow for pops of creaminess, add as a dollop on top of the dish.

Flavor profile: Fatty/hearty, cheesy/creamy

MILK

Milk in ramen? Yes! It adds creaminess, and its dairy flavor takes a back seat in the soup. Leave the 2 percent and skim milk in the fridge, though—they won't add as much body as whole milk. An even creamier option is evaporated milk, which is concentrated and, as a bonus, is shelf stable. You can also replace milk with your favorite vegan option, though I recommend avoiding any low- or nonfat options.

Replace ½ to 1 cup [120 to 240 ml] of water with milk. If using evaporated milk, use half as much. Be careful: milk will cause your soup to foam. Lowering the heat and also adding the noodle cake or other ingredients will help decrease foaming.

Flavor profile: Cheesy/creamy

OIL

There are three types of cooking oil that are most useful for instant ramen: neutral oil, olive oil, and coconut oil. I don't recommend cooking with sesame oil.

We use the term *neutral oil* to describe any oil that does not provide a strong flavor, such as avocado, canola, corn, grape-seed, safflower, sunflower, and vegetable oils. Often, these oils also have higher smoke points, which means they are suitable for high-temperature cooking. These oils are excellent for sautéing, searing, and adding body without overpowering other flavors.

Depending on the olive variety and processing method, extra-virgin olive oil can bring a wide range of fruity, floral, peppery, nutty, and grassy flavors to your ramen. These flavors are particularly noticeable when the oil is uncooked.

Coconut oil is mostly composed of saturated fat, which means that it is solid at room temperature and has a rich texture similar to butter. It has a distinct coconut flavor.

Use 1 to 2 tablespoons for most recipes. You can use 1 teaspoon when only a touch of fat is needed. To sear or sauté food, heat oil in the saucepan over medium-high to high heat during the Pre-Simmer phase. To give your soup extra body, add it at the beginning of the Simmer phase. Olive oil can be drizzled over your ramen at the Finish phase.

Flavor profile: Fatty/hearty

PEANUTS

While they may not be actual nuts (they're legumes), peanuts are used in many cuisines to bring nutty flavors and textural contrast. Use roasted peanuts, which have a more pronounced flavor than the unroasted ones. You can crush them in a mortar and pestle or by putting them in a zip-top bag and gently pressing down with a small pan.

Add 1 to 2 tablespoons, crushed or whole, at the Finish phase.

Flavor profile: Nutty

PEANUT BUTTER

Peanut butter provides fatty, nutty richness to a soup. It's one of the best quick add-ins to give your ramen some thickness, heft, and flavor. Many peanut butters contain additional ingredients such as sugars and oils that can bring additional flavors into your ramen. For pure peanut flavor, look for one that is made only of peanuts or, at most, just peanuts and salt.

Add 1 to 2 tablespoons before anything else at the Simmer phase. Stir until it is completely incorporated into the soup.

Flavor profile: Fatty/hearty, nutty

POTATOES

While there are thousands of varieties of potatoes, they can largely be classified into three groups: starchy (such as russets), waxy (such as red potatoes), and all-purpose (such as Yukon golds). Starchy ones break down and can help thicken your soup. Waxy and all-purpose potatoes both retain their shape, with the former having a firmer texture. Avoid using large chunks of potatoes because they will take too long to cook.

Add ½ to 1 cup [70 to 140 g] (1 or 2 medium potatoes), diced small or thinly sliced into half-moons or quarters, during the Simmer phase and cook for at least 5 minutes or, for roasted flavors, sauté potatoes in 1 tablespoon of fat for 5 minutes or until browned.

Flavor profile: Starchy

RICE CAKES

Known as tteok in Korean cuisine, these chewy cakes are made from rice flour and come in two shapes: cylinders and ovals. It's best to use ovals for your ramen because the cylinders take longer to soften. The dense chewiness of tteok works well as a contrast with the more pliant texture of ramen noodles.

Add 12 to 18 rice cakes (2 to 3 ounces [55 to 85 g]) during the Simmer phase and cook for at least 2 minutes or, if frozen, 3 minutes.

Flavor profile: Starchy

SEMIHARD AND SEMISOFT CHEESES

These are the workhorse cheeses that are popular options at the deli counter, including cheddar, Swiss, mozzarella, and Jack. They work well as toppings and as ingredients in sauces, but they should not be incorporated into your soup because they tend to clump up into chewy bits in hot water.

Add 1 to 2 ounces [30 to 55 g] at the Finish phase. If you are making a saucy (rather than soupy) dish, stir to combine the cheese into the noodles.

Flavor profile: Cheesy/creamy, savory

SESAME SEEDS

A staple in many East Asian cuisines, sesame seeds add a pleasant nuttiness and light crunch. Use toasted sesame seeds, available at any grocery store, not raw ones, because they have a much richer flavor.

Shake on at the Finish phase.

Flavor profile: Nutty

SOFT CHEESES

Soft cheeses, such as Brie, blue, and Camembert, aren't just for spreading on crackers. They melt smoothly, which makes them good ingredients to bring their often funky flavors to your soup.

Add 1 to 2 ounces [30 to 55 g] during the Simmer phase, stirring to incorporate into your soup.

Flavor profile: Cheesy/creamy

SOUR CREAM

This is cream that has been lightly fermented to create a thicker texture and acidic flavor. Don't cook it, as the proteins in the sour cream will curdle, creating a grainy texture.

Add 1 to 3 tablespoons at the Finish phase and stir to incorporate into the soup, or leave a dollop on top as a garnish.

Flavor profile: Cheesy/creamy, acidic

TAHINI

This sesame seed paste can do wonders for your ramen. It not only brings the toasty aromas of sesame seeds but also thickens the soup beautifully. It is one of my favorite ingredients to give instant ramen a decadent, rich texture. If you can find them, Japanese sesame paste (neri goma) and Chinese sesame paste (zhi ma jiang) have bolder, nuttier flavors and can be used the same way.

Add 1 to 2 tablespoons before anything else at the Simmer phase. Stir until it is completely incorporated into the soup.

Flavor profile: Fatty/hearty, nutty

TOASTED SESAME OIL

This dark-hued oil has very strong toasted and nutty flavors. Because of its intensity, it's best not to cook with it and instead use it in moderation as a finishing oil. Note that sometimes it is labeled as "roasted sesame oil."

Use 1 to 2 teaspoons, drizzled at the Finish phase.

Flavor profile: Fatty/hearty, nutty

Aromatic

These are the flavor superheroes—ingredients that can totally reorient the direction and identity of your ramen. The ingredients in this category are typically used in smaller quantities and their main purpose is to provide outsized flavor.

Under this umbrella is quite the motley crew. You have herbs, which are plant leaves, and spices, which can be seeds, bark, or roots. Both herbs and spices bring potent aromas that can define a dish: think about the role of basil in pesto or vanilla in ice cream. Herbs with large leaves such as basil, cilantro, mint, and parsley tend to have more complete flavors when raw or minimally cooked. Spices, on the other hand, often need to be cooked in fat or water to bring their flavors out.

Fiery chile peppers fall under this category as well. Used dried or fresh, they contain capsaicin, which produces a burning sensation that can be appetizing at the right level. Their fieriness can be enhanced by cooking them in fat or water to extract and distribute the capsaicin.

The last group is composed of pungent ingredients. Here, I consider pungency as a "biting" flavor, one that provokes a sharp physical sensation that is distinct from fieriness. All the members of the onion family are pungent (if you've ever tried biting a raw clove of garlic, you know how it bites back), as is ginger and a number of spices such as black pepper and mustard.

AROMATICS AND CUISINE

Aromatics, in combination with other ingredients, have a powerful effect on the identity of your ramen bowl. Just the combination of two ingredients can evoke the flavor profile of a cuisine. See the chart below for some examples.

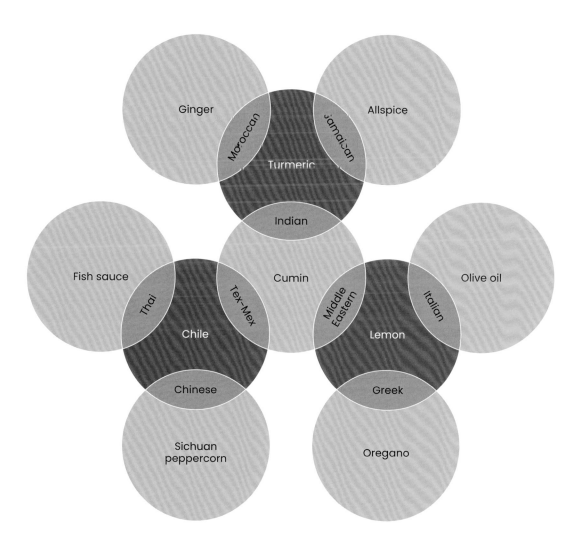

BASIL

The most common variety you'll find is sweet basil, also known as Italian basil. It is a delicate herb that has floral and licorice notes. Thai basil, which can be found in Asian supermarkets, is more sturdy and has a stronger licorice flavor. Don't store basil in the refrigerator—it'll be unhappy and wilt. Instead, keep it on your kitchen counter with the stems partially submerged in water.

Use 5 to 10 leaves. For maximum basil flavor, add raw at the Finish phase. To help release the flavor, give each leaf a pinch or tear the leaves before adding. To infuse your soup with a muted basil flavor, add whole leaves in the Simmer phase.

Flavor profile: Herbal

BERBERE

This spice mix is ubiquitous in Ethiopian cuisine, the flavorful result of generations of history and culture. Ethiopian families often make their own berbere, giving their home cooking its own culinary fingerprint. The backbone of berbere is chile powder, which is then supplemented by twelve or more additional spices. Complex and fiery, it's an excellent ingredient to instantly add a depth of flavor to your ramen.

Add 1 to 3 teaspoons at any point during the Simmer phase or, for more vivid flavor, bloom in fat (see page 40).

Flavor profile: Fiery, spiced

BLACK PEPPER

This spice is common for a reason: it brings a welcome array of flavors that are harmonious with nearly any cuisine. Depending on the variety of black pepper used, it can bring in citrusy, fruity, woody, and floral notes. It's best to use freshly ground pepper for maximum flavor.

Use a generous pinch to ¼ teaspoon, ground. Add at the Finish phase or, for more vivid flavor, bloom in fat (see page 40).

Flavor: Spiced, pungent

CHILI CRISP

This versatile, chunky condiment contains red pepper flakes in oil, bolstered by a number of ingredients that add texture, such as fried garlic or shallots. It brings fieriness, savoriness, fattiness, and crunch to your ramen—all in one fell swoop. Many supermarkets stock it in the Asian ingredient section, and it's also easily found online.

Add 1 to 2 tablespoons at the Finish phase. To infuse more fieriness into the soup, add at any point during the Simmer phase. For a more flavorful alternative to cooking oil, use chili crisp when you are searing or sautéing.

Flavor profile: Fiery, fatty/hearty

CHILES

Fresh chiles bring more vegetal notes than dried versions, as well as an additional textural crunch. Two common varieties that are worth trying are jalapeños for mild fieriness and habaneros for strong fieriness.

Add 1 chile, thinly sliced, during the Simmer phase and cook for at least 2 minutes or, for roasted flavors, sauté in oil. You can also make a quick pickle with the peppers to tame the fieriness and add an acidic note (see page 85).

Flavor profile: Fiery, vegetal

CILANTRO

One of the most commonly used herbs in the world, cilantro is also called *coriander* because it grows from the coriander seed. It brings freshness and citrusy flavors to your ramen. Some people have a genetic variation that makes cilantro taste soapy, though it may be possible to overcome this aversion by eating it repeatedly.

Use 3 to 6 sprigs. Pluck the leaves whole and chop the stems—they're packed with flavor, so don't throw them out. For maximum cilantro flavor, add raw at the Finish phase. To infuse your soup with a muted cilantro flavor, add in the Simmer phase.

Flavor profile: Herbal

CUMIN

This spice is versatile and, like black pepper, is used in cuisines across the world: Cubans use it in mojo, Moroccans keep it in a shaker on the table, and Indians use it extensively in stews. Try cumin in combination with other spices to evoke a diverse range of global flavors.

Use ½ to 1 teaspoon, whole or ground. Add at the beginning of the Simmer phase or, for more vivid flavor, bloom in fat (see page 40).

Flavor profile: Spiced

CURRY POWDER

Curry powder, while not actually used in Indian cuisine, is a useful shortcut to add a range of flavorful spices, including turmeric, cumin, coriander, and fenugreek. The Japanese use curry powder to prepare a number of dishes, including curry ramen and kare, a rich, gravy-based stew.

Use 1 to 2 teaspoons. Add at the beginning of the Simmer phase or, for more vivid flavor, bloom in fat (see page 40).

Flavor profile: Spiced

GARAM MASALA

This is a spice mix that is commonly used across South Asia and typically includes cardamom, coriander, cumin, and cinnamon, among other spices. It's a surprisingly versatile flavor profile that is equally at home on meat as it is in a cake.

Use ¼ to ½ teaspoon. Add at the beginning of the Simmer phase or, for more vivid flavor, bloom in fat (see page 40).

Flavor profile: Spiced

GARLIC

A staple of cuisines the world over, garlic is beloved for its distinctive sulfurous and pungent flavors. These flavors are particularly prominent when it's raw, cut finely, or mashed. Most instant ramen seasoning sachets contain garlic powder, so you're getting garlic flavor no matter what. However, fresh garlic brings a much more potent range of flavors.

I have two preferred ways to peel garlic. With a knife, cut the root off the end of the clove, place it on a cutting board, and give it a quick smack with the flat side of a large knife. Or, to peel a clove with your hands, cut off the root end of the clove and then gently twist the clove back and forth to loosen the skin. The peel should come off easily.

Use 1 to 2 medium cloves. For a more pungent flavor, mince the garlic. For a more balanced flavor, thinly slice the garlic. Add at the beginning of the Simmer phase or, for more vivid flavor, bloom in fat (see page 40). If you let the garlic brown, it'll develop more nutty and bitter flavors.

Flavor profile: Pungent

GINGER

This knobby rhizome, or underground stem, adds a floral, citrusy note to dishes, as well as a pungent zing. Because it has a fibrous texture, it's necessary to cut it down to a smaller size.

Unless the exterior looks coarse or beat up, you don't need to peel ginger. If you do want to peel it, don't use a knife or a peeler—you'll end up wasting a lot of ginger. Instead, use the edge of a spoon to scrape off the skin.

Use 1 to 2 tablespoons grated, shredded, or finely chopped (a 1- to 2-inch [2.5 to 5 cm] length). Add at the beginning of the Simmer phase or, for more vivid flavor, bloom in fat (see page 40). Ginger is excellent pickled as well (see page 85).

Flavor profile: Pungent

GOCHUJANG

This paste of chile peppers, fermented soybeans, and rice adds fieriness, sweetness, and savoriness, as well as a bit of body to your soup. While it is traditionally a backbone of Korean cuisine, it can enrich dishes from a broad array of cuisines.

Add 1 to 3 teaspoons at the beginning of the Simmer phase before adding the noodle cake. Stir until it has completely dissolved into the soup.

Flavor profile: Fiery, salty, sweet

HOT SAUCE

Within the wide world of hot sauces, there are three main types that you'll encounter in the United States. Louisiana-style hot sauce is typically thin, mildly fiery, and very vinegary. Examples include Tabasco, Crystal, and Frank's RedHot. Mexican-style hot sauce is thicker, more fiery, less vinegary (some don't use vinegar at all), and has additional aromatics and spices to round out the flavor. Examples include Tapatío, Cholula, Valentina, and El Yucateco. Sriracha-style hot sauce is thicker, moderately fiery, and garlicky with an almost ketchup-like sweetness.

Add at the Finish phase.

Flavor profile: Fiery, acidic

MUSTARD

This condiment is made from mustard seeds mixed with other, often acidic, ingredients. Mustard seed's pungent punch is found in many cultures, including in Chinese, Indian, and French cuisines. I prefer the clean flavors of Dijon-style mustards, but you can use whatever you have on hand.

Add 1 to 2 teaspoons at any point during the Simmer phase.

Flavor profile: Pungent

ONION

The more watery, sweeter cousin of garlic, onions add pungent sweetness when cooked and a zing when added raw. The high sugar content of onions means they caramelize readily when cooked in fat.

Use ¼ to ½ cup [35 to 70 g], diced (an eighth to a quarter of a large onion). Add at the beginning of the Simmer phase or, for caramelly flavors, sauté in at least 1 teaspoon of fat over medium-high heat for 2 minutes or until browned. For a pungent note, add raw at the Finish phase.

Flavor profile: Pungent

OREGANO

Oregano is one of the few herbs that manages to retain good flavor even when dried. It is frequently used in Mediterranean and Latin cuisines. It is also an acceptable substitute for epazote, an herb used in many traditional Mexican dishes.

Add ¼ to ½ teaspoon at the beginning of the Simmer phase.

Flavor profile: Herbal

PAPRIKA

This spice is created from dried red peppers. It's typically mild and sweet with a gentle pepper flavor, which means it can be used in large quantities without overpowering a dish. Smoked paprika is a popular ingredient in Spanish cuisine, where it is known as *pimentón de la vera*.

Use 1 to 2 teaspoons. Add at the Finish phase or at any point during the Simmer phase or, for more vivid flavor, bloom in fat (see page 40).

Flavor profile: Spiced

PARSLEY

Parsley is the supporting actor of the herb world. It doesn't take center stage, but it has a mild, leafy flavor that balances other flavors and allows it to be used in large quantities.

Use 1 to 2 tablespoons of leaves, finely chopped. Add raw at the Finish phase or, to infuse your soup with mild parsley flavor, add at any point during the Simmer phase.

Flavor profile: Herbal

TIP: QUICKLY SEPARATING LEAVES FROM STEMS

Stick the parsley, stem-side first, into one of the coarse holes of a box grater. Pull the parsley through the grater, and the leaves will come right off.

PESTO

This traditional Italian paste is typically made from basil leaves, olive oil, garlic, pine nuts, and Parmesan cheese, making it an excellent all-in-one package to bring a range of flavors to your soup. If left uncooked, it will have more of a bite from the garlic. Make your own using my quick recipe below or get it premade from the supermarket.

Add 1 to 2 tablespoons at any point during the Simmer phase. For a more pungent and aromatic kick, add a dollop at the Finish phase.

Flavor profile: Herbal, fatty/hearty, pungent

TIP: QUICK PESTO RECIPE

Using a food processor, combine the following ingredients until they form a smooth paste: ½ cup [120 ml] olive oil; 1 garlic clove, split in half; 2 cups [25 g] basil leaves; ½ cup [15 g] grated Parmesan cheese; 2 tablespoons pine nuts; and a generous pinch of salt.

RED PEPPER FLAKES

These dried and pulverized bits of chiles are a quick way to add fieriness to your ramen. The flavor and intensity vary based on the variety of pepper used. (The common "red pepper flakes" you see in pizzerias are a mix of peppers, including cayenne.) Note that red pepper flakes impart a higher level of fieriness when they are cooked in your ramen, as opposed to being added at the end.

Add at the Finish phase or at any point during the Simmer phase or, for more vivid flavor, bloom in fat (see page 40).

Flavor profile: Fiery

SCALLIONS

Known as *negi* in Japan, scallions are an essential component of traditional ramen. Unlike their onion and garlic cousins, scallions won't dominate a dish's flavor profile. Instead, they offer a pleasantly mild onion note, as well as a fresh textural contrast. The white section of the scallion has a sharper flavor while the green section has a more chive-like flavor. Both sections are fine to use interchangeably.

Use ½ to 1 scallion, very thinly sliced. Add at the Finish phase or, to infuse the soup with a mild scallion flavor, double the quantity, chop into larger chunks, and add during the Simmer phase for at least 2 minutes or, for roasted flavors, sauté in oil.

Flavor profile: Pungent

TIP: SCALLION CUTS

Having problems with scallion slices sticking together? The trick to cleanly slicing scallions is to use a sharp, honed knife and to use a slight back-and-forth slicing motion, rather than simply using an up-and-down motion.

SHICHIMI TOGARASHI

If you'd like to add some fieriness to your ramen while remaining true to Japanese flavors, reach for this spice mix of chile powder balanced with sesame, citrus, seaweed, and other spices. Also known simply as shichimi, it instantly broadens the flavors of any dish and is commonly found as a condiment in ramen restaurants.

Add at the Finish phase.

Flavor profile: Fiery, nutty

SICHUAN PEPPERCORNS

This berry (which is unrelated to the black peppercorn) contains compounds that create a unique buzzing sensation in the mouth. Combined with the fiery flavor of chile peppers, it creates a feeling that the Chinese refer to as *mala*, which means "spicy and numbing." It also imparts a citrus-like flavor.

Use ½ to 1 teaspoon, ground. Add at the beginning of the Simmer phase or, for more vivid flavor, bloom in fat (see page 40).

Flavor profile: Spiced, pungent

STAR ANISE

This distinctively shaped fruit has a strong anise flavor, similar to fennel and licorice. It is often paired with soy sauce, bringing warmth and sweetness. It's too woody to be eaten.

Use 1 to 2 whole pods. Add at the beginning of the Simmer phase. You can leave it as a decorative element or remove it before eating.

Flavor profile: Spiced

TAJÍN

Tajín is a popular Mexican spice mix that brings together dried chiles with dehydrated lime. It's a convenient way to punch up flavors in your instant ramen with a few shakes.

Add at the Finish phase.

Flavor profile: Fiery, acidic, salty

THAI CURRY PASTE

If you're looking for a shortcut to complex flavors, Thai curry pastes are an excellent option. They are packed with highly aromatic ingredients such as garlic, lemongrass, cilantro, and chiles. There are numerous varieties, but the most common ones—in order of fieriest to mildest—are green, red, and yellow.

Add 1 to 2 tablespoons at any point during the Simmer phase, stirring to incorporate it into the soup.

Flavor profile: Spiced, fiery, salty

THYME

This herb is particularly beloved in Mediterranean and Middle Eastern cuisines. It also holds a central place in French cuisine as a main component of the bouquet garni, which is used to flavor French stocks and broths. It contributes herbal, minty, and earthy flavors.

Use 2 to 4 sprigs of fresh thyme or 1 to 2 teaspoons of dried thyme leaves. Add at the beginning of the Simmer phase or, for more vivid flavor, infuse in fat (see page 40).

Flavor profile: Herbal

Leftovers, Cup Ramen, and Beyond

Instant ramen is a playground for leftovers. Almost anything can be repurposed as an add-in or topping. Here are some thought starters:

- **Salsas, chutneys, and other condiments** can be drizzled on at the end.

- **Dumplings** only need to be warmed up during the last 30 seconds of the Simmer phase.

- **Prepared grains** can bulk out your dish. Try adding ½ to 1 cup [70 to 140 g] during the Simmer phase.

- **Kebabs, rotisserie chicken, and other meats** make good toppings. Add them cold or warm them briefly during the Simmer phase.

- **Cold salads and dips** can be toppings for drained noodles.

- **Ethiopian wats, Indian curries, West African soups, and other stewy dishes** can be good foundations—replace 1 cup [240 ml] of water with the stew and decrease the seasoning sachet as needed.

- **Chinese takeout, veggie side dishes, and other stir-fries and sautés** can be dropped right into the soup during the Simmer phase.

Not feeling soupy? If you decide to drain your noodles (see page 50), here are a few quick dressing ideas that work well. Combine the ingredients as noted below, mix with the noodles, and then finish with a few dashes of the seasoning sachet in the same way you would use salt to taste. Then top your noodles with fresh veggies or whatever you'd like, just as you would with soupy noodles.

These recipes will make around 2 tablespoons of dressing, which I find is a good amount for one packet of instant ramen noodles. If you want more, simply increase the volume while maintaining the same ratios. If you have extra dressing left, you can always use it on a sandwich or salad—or your next bowl of instant ramen.

DRESSING RATIOS

Barbecue vinaigrette

Chili crisp vinaigrette

Gochujang mayo

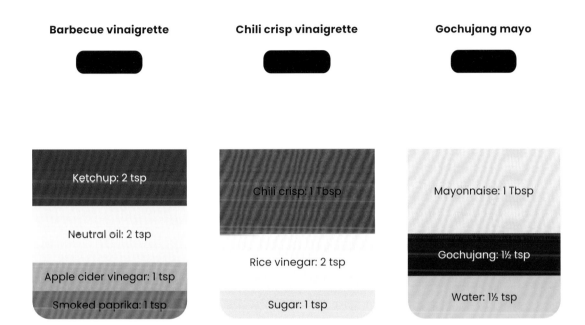

Ketchup: 2 tsp

Neutral oil: 2 tsp

Apple cider vinegar: 1 tsp

Smoked paprika: 1 tsp

Chili crisp: 1 Tbsp

Rice vinegar: 2 tsp

Sugar: 1 tsp

Mayonnaise: 1 Tbsp

Gochujang: 1½ tsp

Water: 1½ tsp

Honey mustard dressing

Chile-lime dressing

Honey: 2 tsp

Mustard: 2 tsp

Neutral oil: 2 tsp

Water: 2 tsp

Hot sauce: 1 Tbsp

Neutral oil: 1 Tbsp

Lime juice: 1½ tsp

DRESSING RATIOS (cont'd)

Miso dressing

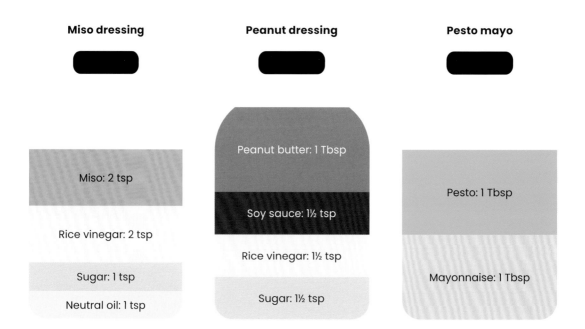

Miso: 2 tsp

Rice vinegar: 2 tsp

Sugar: 1 tsp

Neutral oil: 1 tsp

Peanut dressing

Peanut butter: 1 Tbsp

Soy sauce: 1½ tsp

Rice vinegar: 1½ tsp

Sugar: 1½ tsp

Pesto mayo

Pesto: 1 Tbsp

Mayonnaise: 1 Tbsp

Soy dressing

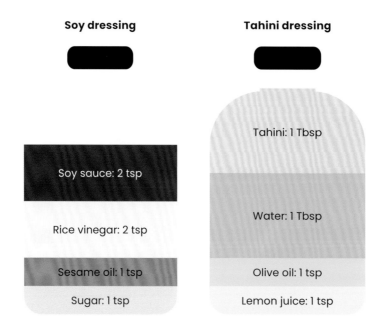

Soy sauce: 2 tsp

Rice vinegar: 2 tsp

Sesame oil: 1 tsp

Sugar: 1 tsp

Tahini dressing

Tahini: 1 Tbsp

Water: 1 Tbsp

Olive oil: 1 tsp

Lemon juice: 1 tsp

Cup Ramen

This book is mostly about cup ramen's cousin, packet instant ramen, but I would be remiss to not have anything about this wildly popular product, which can come in a cup or bowl shape and was first developed with Cup Noodles by Nissin Food Products.

As convenient as they may be, cup ramens are not a particularly exciting topic for a cookbook because their whole reason for existence is to eliminate the need to do anything. Nonetheless, there are some easy ways to build on cup ramens that remain true to its spirit and don't require pulling out a cutting board or turning on the stove.

There are three main things you can do with added ingredients in a cup ramen:

- **Cook or warm up ingredients by adding them to the cup before adding boiling water or before microwaving.** Options include frozen small-cut vegetables, tteok (Korean rice cakes), spices, precooked meats and sausages, and a beaten egg. To add an egg, crack it directly into the cup and beat it using a fork or chopsticks. Don't try to cook or warm anything else alongside it, or it won't cook fully.

- **Mix in ingredients, once the noodles are done cooking, to add flavor or body to your cup ramen.** Options include neutral oil, butter, tahini and nut butters, tomato paste, cream, and miso.

- **Top the cup ramen with ingredients that bring additional flavors and textures.** Options include herbs, cheese, sesame seeds, canned fish, canned beans, or any condiments such as mayonnaise or ketchup.

BEAN CHILI
Recommended cup: Beef flavor

Cook with ¼ cup [35 g] of canned, drained black, pinto, or red beans; 1 tablespoon of tomato paste; and 1 teaspoon of chili powder.

Mix in 1 teaspoon of neutral oil such as sunflower oil.

Top with shredded cheddar cheese.

BREAKFAST IN A CUP
Recommended cup: Any

Cook with 1 egg, beaten in the cup.

Mix in 10 pieces of pepperoni (about ½ ounce [15 g]).

Top with 1 slice of American cheese.

BROCCOLI MAC 'N' CHEESE
Recommended cup: Chicken flavor

Cook with ¼ cup [35 g] of frozen broccoli florets, then drain.

Mix in 2 slices of American cheese.

BUDAE JJIGAE JR.
Recommended cup: Shin Cup or other spicy Korean-style ramen

Cook with 1 teaspoon of gochujang and 10 pieces of tteok. Only add half of the seasoning sachet.

Mix in 10 pieces of pepperoni (about ½ ounce [15 g]).

Top with ¼ cup [35 g] of sliced kimchi.

CACIO E PEPE

Recommended cup: Chicken flavor

Cook with a generous pinch of black pepper, then drain.

Mix in 1 tablespoon of unsalted butter, 2 tablespoons of grated Pecorino Romano, and a splash of hot water.

CREAMY CHICKEN

Recommended cup: Chicken flavor

Cook with ¼ cup [35 g] of frozen peas and carrots.

Mix in 1 tablespoon of heavy cream.

Top with shredded rotisserie chicken or cold-cut chicken.

ELOTE

Recommended cup: Shin Cup or other spicy Korean-style ramen

Cook normally, then drain.

Top with 1 tablespoon of mayonnaise, ¼ cup [35 g] of canned corn, cotija cheese, seasoning sachet, and, if desired, a lime wedge and cilantro leaves.

MEDITERRANEAN FISH

Recommended cup: Shrimp flavor

Cook with 1 tablespoon of tomato paste and a pinch of thyme.

Mix in 1 teaspoon of extra-virgin olive oil.

Top with 1 canned sardine fillet and lemon juice.

MAPO

Recommended cup: Any

Cook with ½ teaspoon of ground Sichuan peppercorns and ¼ cup [35 g] of silken tofu.

Mix in 1 tablespoon of chili crisp or chili oil.

MASALA MATAR
Recommended cup: Chicken flavor

Cook with a generous pinch of garam masala, 1 tablespoon of tomato paste, and ¼ cup [35 g] of frozen peas.

Mix in 3 tablespoons of coconut milk.

MISO CORN
Recommended cup: Any

Cook with 1 teaspoon of miso.

Top with 1 tablespoon of unsalted butter and ¼ cup [35 g] of canned corn

SESAME-PEANUT
Recommended cup: Any

Cook normally.

Mix in 2 tablespoons of tahini and 1 teaspoon of rice vinegar.

Top with roasted, salted peanuts.

PART II

Ramen Concepts

What Should

I Cook?

About the Concepts

Here you will find forty-one concepts that can take your instant ramen in new, surprising, and delicious directions. I'm calling them *concepts* rather than *recipes* because I want you to think of them more as templates, to be used as jumping-off points for your own creative experimentation. I've organized them loosely as soups, stews, and saucy dishes. I use the word *loosely* because there's really more of a spectrum between the categories—I think of soups as being more liquidy, stews as being more chunky and thick, and if the liquid gets thick enough to cling to the noodles, I consider it saucy. Start by following the concept as written, and then make it your own! Switch up the ingredients, try new cooking methods, and discover new flavor combinations. For each concept, I've included a few "try this" thought starters.

In the spirit of harnessing the ease and simplicity of cooking with instant ramen, I adhered to the following principles in developing these concepts:

- **Everything can be made in one pot.** You will never need to turn on more than one burner.

- **Everything can be made in 20 minutes or less.** People cook at different speeds, of course, but I manage to do each one, start to finish, within this window. Exceptions to this rule apply to the make-ahead recipes, such as Chashu Bacon (page 157), and the Spinach Ramen Gratin (page 227), which is the only concept that uses the oven.

- **All components of the instant ramen packet are used.**
  I don't see the point of using only the noodles or the seasoning sachet. You can always purchase seasonings or
  plain noodles if you prefer to use only one or the other.

- **There are a maximum of ten ingredients, in addition to
  the packet of instant ramen itself.** I do not include salt or
  water in this count.

- **All required ingredients are commonly available in
  supermarkets.** There are a handful of optional ingredients that will require online ordering or a visit to a
  specialty store.

Applying these restrictions, I developed each concept with
extreme minimalism in mind, focusing on the essential flavors of
each dish and paring away everything else. I've also concocted
some tricks to speed up the process when some of these dishes
would normally take hours.

As a result, I would not consider any of these concepts to be "authentic" or "traditional" versions of their respective dishes. They are highly simplified and have been adapted for instant ramen. Many Italians would never put chicken seasoning in their aglio e olio pasta, the way my approach does. Japanese tonkotsu usually requires hours of simmering, while mine comes together in a few minutes. Vietnamese pho recipes can easily have twenty-five or more ingredients, while mine uses just ten. And so on.

Thanks to the power of instant ramen, these dishes may be simplified, but they are absolutely tasty. And that is what the instant ramen kitchen is all about: maximum creativity, maximum deliciousness, and minimum effort.

Getting Creative

Once you've gotten into the swing of things building off of my concepts, I hope you will be inspired to start blazing your own instant ramen trail.

But what happens if you feel stuck trying to think of how to come up with your instant ramen concept? I am a big believer in the power of constraints to turbocharge creativity. If you look back at most innovations in art, cuisine, and technology, you will more often than not find that they were born out of constraints. As noted earlier, the invention of instant ramen itself was the product of challenging, impoverished circumstances in postwar Japan.

Try two different exercises in imposing constraints on your creative process and see whether it helps: **1** pick one ingredient to build around or **2** pick one dish to build toward.

Starting with an Ingredient

What you currently have in your refrigerator and pantry is a constraint—it's a limited universe of options. The trick is to find a way to commit to one ingredient that will then inform how you build out your bowl of ramen. Use the constraint of that one ingredient as your north star to pick anything else you'd like to add.

Try the following:

- **Pick an ingredient you have not used in a long time.** We all have those things that, for some reason, we just never seem to use. Maybe it's a bottle of fish sauce gathering dust in your pantry or a jar of curry paste that seems to have made a permanent home in your refrigerator. If you see it and you feel that pang, knowing it's gone unused for too long, grab it and build your ramen around it.

- **Pick an ingredient that you're most excited about.** Did you just pick up some beautiful mushrooms that you can't wait to eat? Or maybe you have a pack of bacon that's calling out to be fried. Make that exciting ingredient the focal point of your ramen.

- **Pick an ingredient that's about to go bad.** Scan through your kitchen to see whether there's an ingredient that really *ought* to be used right away. Anchor your ramen around that ingredient so that it doesn't go to waste.

Starting with a Dish

Another path to creativity is to start by visualizing a final dish. It could be inspired by a beloved comfort food from your childhood or simply something you're craving in the moment.

Sure, you can peruse a few recipes online, but focus on leaning into your intuition. Think about the key characteristics of that dish and try ingredients that bring out those flavors. My own recipe concepts in this book are a result of applying this thinking. Even if the end result doesn't quite resemble your initial vision, it's quite likely you'll enjoy eating it.

As I stated previously, don't limit yourself to imagining Asian dishes. Instant ramen can be used to make all kinds of stews, soups, and noodle dishes—no matter the cuisine. In some cases, it results in a curious new twist on a dish, especially if it's one that isn't typically eaten with noodles. Borscht, for example, is given a very different identity with instant ramen. Fortunately, I've found that instant ramen noodles fit well in a wide variety of cuisines and dishes. To emphasize this point, my own recipe concepts are inspired by food cultures from around the world.

So, let's imagine you have an aunt who makes an incredible spinach lasagna, and you'd like to try to make an instant ramen version of that. What might you think about adding to the saucepan? Spinach, of course. Maybe some Italian sausage, some fennel, some oregano, some canned crushed tomatoes, and a blanket of mozzarella to finish?

In this case, choosing your aunt's spinach lasagna has become your creative constraint. Now you need to use your imagination to bring its flavors into your instant ramen . . . and then taste what happens!

Almost all of the ramen recipes in this book serve one person as a complete meal. If supplemented by other dishes, they can generally serve two as a main.

You can double most of these recipes so they serve two people as a complete meal or four people as a side. I do not recommend trying to scale up these recipes beyond that. To double a recipe, you have three options:

- Double the ingredients and use a wider pot instead of a saucepan to make the dish. This is the easiest method but it can be difficult to portion out for each person.

- Cook the noodles separately. For the soup, decrease the water by ½ cup [120 ml] per portion. Having the noodles separate makes portioning easier. However, this will not work for any preparation that results in saucy or dry noodles, such as the Cacio e Pepe Ramen (page 218) or Ramen Fideuà (page 223).

- Use two saucepans and make two portions simultaneously.

WHAT SHOULD I COOK?*

*Heavily inspired by a flowchart in Samin Nosrat's excellent book *Salt, Fat, Acid, Heat*.

How soon do you want to eat?

ASAP!

Basic ramen—it takes just minutes and is super versatile. Also try the Cacio e Pepe Ramen (page 218), Egg Drop Ramen (page 166), or Ramen alla Marinara (page 220).

I've got 20 minutes max.

Which flavor profile sounds good?

RICH

. . . and nutty

Peanut-y

Mafe is a satisfying stew from West Africa (Mafe Ramen, page 192).

Sesame-y

Tantanmen (page 208) covers a lot of flavor bases with pork, chile, and vinegar.

. . . and cheesy

Spinach Ramen Gratin (page 227) and Mac 'n' Cheese Ramen (page 224) are both gooey delights.

FIERY

. . . and tingly

Yes

Do you like tofu?

I am a tofuhead.

Mapo Tofu Ramen (page 211) brings a hefty buzz from Sichuan peppercorns.

Not this time.

Xi'an-Style Cumin Lamb Ramen (page 212) has some buzz too, but balanced with other flavors.

No

. . . and hearty

Chinese

Egg Drop Ramen (page 166) is the move.

Korean

Budae Jjigae (page 204) is a party of meat and cheese.

Colombian

Ajiáco Ramen (page 183) has a potato-fortified soup that'll stick to your ribs.

Breakfast

B.E.C. Ramen (page 228) will fuel you up for the day.

. . . and creamy

OK, are you basically looking for tonkotsu?

Yep

I figured. Then make Fukuoka-Style Tonkotsu Ramen (page 152), of course!

No

Beef Stroganoff Ramen (page 195) is pure creamy comfort in a bowl.

Sour

Kimchi Jjigae Ramen (page 207) is one of my all-time favorites.

Cheesy

Cheesy Buldak Ramen (page 234) will make you sweat.

Creamy

Thai Green Curry Ramen (page 200) balances the heat with coconut milk.

Meaty

Sega Wat Ramen (page 235) is my go-to for meaty deliciousness.

PLANT-FORWARD

Do you want it hot or cold?

Hot

Which plant?

Green beans
Fasolia Ramen (page 187) is an ode to this veggie.

Tomatoes
Tomato and Egg Stir-Fry Ramen (page 171) is a Chinese comfort favorite.

Beans
Frijoles de la Olla Ramen (page 180) is for legume lovers.

Zucchini
Couscous Ramen (page 191) beautifully showcases this ingredient.

Peppers
Shakshuka Ramen (page 188) provides a double dose via sliced bell peppers and paprika.

Garlic all day
Aglio e Olio Ramen (page 217) is as garlicky as it gets.

A bit of everything
Soupe au Pistou Ramen (page 176) can take any veggie you throw at it.

Cold

Soupy
Naengmyeon Ramen (page 176) is the perfect ice-cold dish for a hot day.

Not soupy
Bibim Guksu Ramen (page 231) is basically a refreshing ramen salad.

BALANCED

Do you have time to do some make-ahead toppings?

Yep
Try Classic Shio Ramen (page 149), Tokyo-Style Shoyu Ramen (page 150), or Sapporo-Style Butter Miso Ramen (page 151)—three traditional Japanese styles with a nice array of flavorful toppings.

Nope

Southeast Asian
Pho Ramen (page 172) hits the right balance of sweet, fresh, and meaty.

South Asian
Coconut Chicken Ramen (page 203) is like a warm hug.

Cantonese
Wonton Soup Ramen (page 167) is a harmonious meeting of noodles and dumplings.

COMPLEX

How do you feel about seafood?

Yum!

Soupy
Moqueca Ramen (page 184) is a riff on one of the great seafood stews of the world.

Dry
Ramen Fideuà (page 223) is like ramen paella—crispy bottom and all. You've never had ramen like this.

Meh.

Aloo Gobi Ramen (page 199) gets its complexity from garam masala.

Borscht Ramen (page 196) brings together diverse flavors into one harmonious bowl.

SAUCY

Are you going East or West?

East

Black sauce
Jjajangmyeon (page 232) is a super savory street food treat.

Brown sauce
Kare Ramen (page 237) has a sweet and spicy gravy that will soothe your soul.

West

Red sauce
Ramen alla Marinara (page 220) is a surprisingly good riff on a timeless classic.

White sauce
Cacio e Pepe Ramen (page 218) is simple, creamy, and delicious.

Yellow sauce
Carbonara-ish Ramen (page 219) is my *heavily* twisted version of the Italian classic.

Classic Ramen, Improvised

Noodles in an Instant

Before we go any further, if you are desperate for a bowl of noodles, then stop here. This first recipe will take you where you need to go. I call this "Basic Ramen." If you're hungry and want a satisfying meal *now*, this is a great place to start. It's a template for creating a well-rounded bowl of instant ramen in the shortest amount of time possible. The final bowl has protein and vegetables, and the flavor is balanced by some richness in the soup and a pop of acidity from pickles.

There are no make-ahead components, and there's hardly much prep needed, all of which can easily be done in the time it takes for you to heat up the water. To speed things up, I also skip the Pre-Simmer phase.

Timing myself from the moment I walk into the kitchen, I can have a bowl of Basic Ramen on the table and ready to eat in 6½ minutes flat. Try to beat my time!

Basic Ramen

2 cups [475 ml] water

1 egg

One 3½ to 4½ oz [100 to 125 g] packet instant ramen (any flavor)

1 Tbsp fat (like chili crisp, oil, lard, or butter)

1 cup [140 g] fresh or frozen vegetables (like peas, broccoli, kale, or bell peppers, thinly sliced)

2 oz [55 g] precooked or ground meat (like 1 hot dog, sliced; 1 thick slice of SPAM; ground beef; or 1 canned sardine fillet)

Fresh topping (like ½ scallion, thinly sliced, or a few leaves of herbs, optional)

Pickled topping (like a spoonful of kimchi, Beni Shoga [page 156], or sliced cucumber pickles, optional)

SIMMER Bring the water to a simmer over medium-high heat. Crack the egg directly into the water. Then add the seasoning sachet, fat, vegetables, meat, and noodle cake. Gently jiggle the noodle cake to immerse it in the soup. Simmer for 2 minutes or until the noodles are at your desired doneness.

FINISH Pour the ramen into a bowl and top with the fresh topping and/or pickled topping, if using. Serve immediately

TRY THIS Add other finishes such as American cheese, furikake, or crushed peanuts.

For a heartier soup, replace the fat with 2 tablespoons of nut butter or tahini. Add it before the egg and stir to incorporate it into the soup.

The Big Four

There are at least three foundational styles of traditional ramen in Japan: shio (salt), shoyu (soy sauce), and miso. Tonkotsu, considered by some to be the fourth, rounds out the list. Each of these is defined by their tare, a concentrated sauce that provides a distinctive flavor profile to the ramen soup. Due to its pivotal role, it's not unusual for a tare recipe to be considered a closely guarded secret. However, in all cases, the key ingredient in the tare will be salt, soy sauce, or miso based on the style of ramen being created.

The body of the soup comes from a rich stock made from long-simmered bones and aromatics. Collagen from the bones thickens the stock while fat adds creaminess. Tonkotsu uses an extra-rich stock made from pork bones and pork fat—so rich that it is opaque and milky in appearance.

It is a fool's errand to think we can fully recreate traditional ramen using instant ramen. Nonetheless, with a few tricks and flourishes, we can create instant ramen bowls that effectively evoke each style—and taste absolutely delicious.

Traditional ramen wouldn't be the same without its toppings: chashu pork, a soft-cooked egg, and menma (seasoned bamboo shoots), to name a few. Unfortunately, there's no "instant" recipe for these components, so I've included some simple make-ahead recipes. As a result, if you decide to make the toppings, it will require more planning and time commitment than any of the other recipes in the book. It still amounts to a small fraction of the time needed to make traditional ramen, and the results are certainly worth the effort.

If you're pressed for time, you can skip the make-ahead toppings and use these recipes to make the soups, topping your bowls with whatever you have on hand.

Classic Shio Ramen

RECOMMENDED RAMEN:
Chicken-Flavored Classic

Shio, which means "salt" in Japanese, derives most of its salinity from, well, salt. Without soy sauce or miso's complex flavors in the tare, the flavor of the stock becomes more prominent. I use premade chicken broth. In combination with the seasoning sachet, this creates a particularly flavorful, chicken-forward soup. Use the highest quality broth you can find because it will define the flavor of your bowl.

One ¼ oz [7 g] packet powdered gelatin

2 cups [475 ml] low-sodium chicken broth

1 Tbsp lard or neutral oil such as sunflower oil

2 Tbsp mirin

One 3 to 3½ oz [85 to 100 g] packet instant ramen

2 pieces Chashu Bacon (page 157)

2 Tbsp Menma (page 158)

½ scallion, very thinly sliced

1 Ajitsuke Tamago (Jammy Egg, page 160)

Rayu (chili oil, page 159)

3 pieces roasted nori, cut down to ¼ of a full-size nori sheet

PRE-SIMMER In a measuring cup or bowl, add the gelatin to the chicken broth and stir to combine. Let the gelatin bloom for at least 1 minute.

Add the lard and mirin to a medium saucepan over medium high heat. Once the mirin is simmering, cook for 1 minute or until it has reduced to a thicker consistency. Add the broth and seasoning sachet, and stir again.

SIMMER Once the soup is simmering, add the noodle cake and cook for 2 minutes or until your desired doneness.

FINISH Pour the ramen and soup into a bowl. Top it with the chashu, menma, scallion, and jammy egg. Drizzle rayu around the bowl. Add the nori and serve immediately.

TRY THIS For a bright citrus note, add the zest and juice of ¼ lemon as a finish.

For a Hakodate-style shio ramen, add a handful of baby spinach with 30 seconds left in the Simmer phase.

Add 1 tablespoon of minced ginger with the lard and mirin.

Tokyo-Style Shoyu Ramen

RECOMMENDED RAMEN:
Chicken-
Flavored
Classic

This ramen style gets its dark brown hue from the soy sauce in its tare. It's especially popular in the Tokyo region, where it is often made from pork and chicken stock. I've found that the best way to quickly achieve a good depth of flavor with instant ramen is to use leftover chashu liquid, which has all the key components of a shoyu tare and has the added advantage of bringing pork flavor notes.

One ¼ oz [7 g] packet powdered gelatin

1½ cups [360 ml] water

½ cup [120 ml] leftover Chashu Liquid (page 157)

One 3 to 3½ oz [85 to 100 g] packet instant ramen

2 pieces Chashu Bacon (page 157)

2 Tbsp Menma (page 158)

½ scallion, very thinly sliced

1 Ajitsuke Tamago (Jammy Egg, page 160)

3 slices narutomaki (Japanese rice cakes)

3 pieces roasted nori, cut down to ¼ of a full-size nori sheet

PRE-SIMMER In a measuring cup or bowl, add the gelatin to the water and stir to combine. Let the gelatin bloom for at least 1 minute.

Add the water, chashu liquid, and half of the seasoning sachet to a medium saucepan over medium-high heat. Stir again.

SIMMER Once the soup is simmering, add the noodle cake and cook for 2 minutes or until your desired doneness.

FINISH Pour the ramen into a bowl. Top it with the chashu, menma, scallion, jammy egg, and narutomaki. Add the nori last and serve immediately.

TRY THIS

If you don't have chashu liquid, increase the water to 2 cups [475 ml] and add 1 tablespoon of soy sauce and 1 tablespoon of lard or chicken fat.

For an Asahikawa-style bowl, top the ramen with 1 tablespoon or more of lard or chicken fat.

Add a pickle, such as Beni Shoga (page 156) or umeboshi (Japanese pickled plum available at specialty grocery stores).

Sapporo-Style Butter Miso Ramen with Soy-Caramel Mushrooms

Miso ramen hails originally from the northern Japanese island of Sapporo, where its cloudy broth occasionally is fortified with butter and corn. Instead of the usual slabs of chashu, I like making this one with soy-caramel mushrooms, which provide a sweetness and earthiness that I find is excellent for balancing the deep savoriness of the soup. The bowl is rounded out by bean sprouts, which are a must in any Sapporo-style ramen.

One ¼ oz [7 g] packet powdered gelatin

2 cups [475 ml] water

1 Tbsp unsalted butter

2 Tbsp mirin

1 Tbsp miso

One 3 to 3½ oz [85 to 100 g] packet instant ramen

1 cup [100 g] mung bean sprouts

2 Tbsp Menma (page 158)

2 Tbsp canned corn

¼ cup [60 ml] Soy-Caramel Mushrooms (page 161)

PRE-SIMMER In a measuring cup or bowl, add the gelatin to the water and stir to combine. Let the gelatin bloom for at least 1 minute.

Add half of the butter and the mirin to a medium saucepan over medium-high heat. Once the mirin is simmering, cook for 1 minute or until it has reduced to a thicker consistency. Add the water, miso, and half of the seasoning sachet and stir to incorporate the miso into the soup.

SIMMER Once the soup is simmering, add the bean sprouts and noodle cake and cook for 2 minutes or until your desired doneness.

FINISH Pour the ramen into a bowl. Top it with the menma, canned corn, and mushrooms. Add the remaining butter last and serve immediately.

TRY THIS

For a spicy miso ramen, add 1 teaspoon or more of red pepper flakes with the butter and mirin at the Pre-Simmer phase. Drizzle with chili oil as a Finish.

Use different kinds of miso. Darker misos have been fermented for a longer period of time and tend to have bolder flavors.

Fukuoka-Style Tonkotsu Ramen

Ah, tonkotsu: the cool kid in the American ramen world, with its long-simmered, luxurious, creamy broth. It has swept the country, to the point of nearly over-shadowing other options on the ramen menu. This style originated in Fukuoka in southwestern Japan, where it is often served with minimal toppings.

Tonkotsu is traditionally made with pork stock. However, pork-flavored instant ramen is difficult to find, so I typically use the beef-flavored variety, which works well. To approximate tonkotsu's rich texture, I combine a generous amount of gelatin and fat with a touch of milk to create a soup with a surprising level of creaminess and body.

1½ cups [360 ml] water

Two ¼ oz [7 g] packets powdered gelatin

One 3 to 3½ oz [85 to 100 g] packet instant ramen

1½ Tbsp lard

½ cup [120 ml] whole milk

2 slices Chashu Bacon (page 157)

1 Tbsp Beni Shoga (page 156)

1 scallion, thinly sliced (see page 118)

PRE-SIMMER Add the water to a medium saucepan. Add the gelatin to the water and stir to combine. Let the gelatin bloom for at least 1 minute. Heat the saucepan over medium-high heat, add the seasoning sachet and lard, and stir again.

SIMMER Once the soup is simmering, add the noodle cake and milk. Cook for 2 minutes or until your desired doneness.

FINISH Pour the ramen into a bowl. Top it with the chashu, beni shoga, and scallion. Serve immediately.

TRY THIS

Add more ramen top-pings, such as a Jammy Egg (page 160) or nori (see page 94).

Combine tonkotsu with one of the other styles. Make it a shoyu tonkotsu by replac-ing ½ cup [120 ml] of water with ½ cup [120 ml] of chashu liquid or a miso tonkotsu by adding 1 tablespoon of miso. In both cases, decrease the seasoning to half a sachet.

Toppings

If the soup and noodles are the foundation of traditional Japanese ramen, the toppings are the structure on top that provides each bowl's distinctive aesthetics, textures, and personality.

While there is a stricter canon for what can be done with the soup and noodles, nearly anything goes when it comes to the toppings. In certain ramen shops in Japan, you can find toppings such as shaved cheese, duck confit, gooey natto (fermented soybeans), tomatoes, or even fresh fruit such as peaches or pineapple. The diversity of toppings reflects different regional styles, as well as the creativity of each ramen chef.

Included in the next few pages are certain toppings that are near-ubiquitous across Japan and are essential if you want to serve a proper bowl of traditional ramen. You'll find my versions of recipes for a selection of these toppings, using only commonly found ingredients. For example, my Soy-Caramel Mushrooms (page 161) uses button mushrooms instead of wood ear mushrooms, which aren't generally available in mainstream supermarkets.

Each recipe will make enough for at least four servings. One good strategy is to make some of these over the weekend, which will allow you to quickly assemble the final dish for dinner on busier weeknights.

Beni Shoga

Pickled Ginger

Beni shoga brings pops of pungency, acidity, and bright red to the bowl. It's traditionally made with young ginger and vinegar made from ume, a Japanese plum. However, I've found that this recipe, which uses normal ginger and red wine vinegar, produces an excellent pickle to use on your ramen. I add a bit of red food coloring to give the pickle its characteristic hue.

4 oz [115 g] knob ginger (about 6 in [15.25 cm] length), peeled and julienned

1 tsp salt

2 tsp sugar

¼ cup [60 ml] red wine vinegar

3 drops red food coloring (optional)

Combine all the ingredients in a bowl and stir well. Refrigerate for at least 3 hours before using. Stir again before serving. Store in an airtight container in the refrigerator for up to 6 months.

TRY THIS　Use different kinds of vinegars, such as apple cider vinegar or rice vinegar, to create new flavor profiles.

Chashu Bacon
Soy-Braised Bacon

The most common protein you'll see on traditional Japanese ramen is chashu, pork belly braised in sweet soy sauce until tender. It's highly flavorful and tender enough to not require a knife, making it an excellent topping for ramen. Instead of using plain pork belly, I like using bacon, which is pork belly that's been cured and smoked. Bacon is easier to find, and I like the smokiness that it brings to ramen.

Don't throw out that chashu liquid! It can be reused for more chashu, to marinate jammy eggs, or to make shoyu ramen.

CHASHU LIQUID
½ cup [120 ml] soy sauce

¼ cup [50 g] sugar

¼ cup [60 ml] mirin

1½ cups [360 ml] water, plus more as needed

1 in [2.5 cm] knob ginger, sliced

BACON
1 lb [455 g] bacon, divided into three equal portions

Toothpicks

TO MAKE THE CHASHU LIQUID: Place all the ingredients in a bowl and stir to combine.

TO MAKE THE BACON: For each portion of bacon, roll up one slice into a spiral, then roll another slice around that, another slice around that, and so on, until you've used all the slices. Secure the roll with two toothpicks inserted slightly off-center in the roll. Repeat with the other two portions of bacon.

Heat a 10-inch [25 cm] pot over medium-high heat. Add the bacon rolls to the pan and sear on all sides for 5 to 7 minutes or until browned all over.

Lay the rolls flat in the pot and add the chashu liquid. Add more water if needed to bring the liquid at least halfway up the rolls. Bring to a simmer and then lower the heat to low. Simmer for 30 to 45 minutes, flipping the rolls at least once halfway through the cook time, until they are tender.

Transfer the chashu rolls and liquid to a container and refrigerate for at least 1 hour and up to 1 week. Slice each roll horizontally to make six total chashu bacon rolls. Remove the toothpicks before serving.

TRY THIS For tofu, drain and slice 1 lb [455 g] of extra-firm tofu. Coat with 2 tablespoons of neutral oil and bake at 450°F [230°C] for 30 minutes or until browned. Simmer in the chashu liquid for 30 minutes.

For chicken, sear 1 lb [455 g] of boneless, skinless chicken thighs in 1 tablespoon of neutral oil for 5 minutes or until browned all over. Simmer in the chashu liquid for 30 minutes to 1 hour or until tender.

Menma

Seasoned Bamboo Shoots

Menma is a common ramen topping made from bamboo shoots. You can find them ready-to-eat in Japanese specialty stores. It's also easy to make menma at home. While this version is not fermented like traditional menma, it is still a delicious addition to your ramen.

Note that the quality of canned bamboo shoots varies widely. Some brands have an off-putting aroma that makes them unusable. Open the can and give it a sniff. I have found that La Choy bamboo shoots tend to work well.

One 8 oz [230 g] can bamboo shoots, preferably La Choy brand, drained and rinsed

1 Tbsp soy sauce

2 tsp sugar

1 tsp sesame oil

Add the bamboo shoots to a small or medium saucepan and cover with water. Heat over high heat until boiling. Boil for 3 minutes and then drain. Return the saucepan to the stovetop over medium-low heat. Add the soy sauce and sugar. Simmer until the liquid has mostly evaporated, about 3 minutes. Add the sesame oil and stir to combine. Use immediately or refrigerate for up to 1 week.

TRY THIS Give the menma some brightness by adding 1 tablespoon or more of vinegar along with the soy sauce and sugar. Increase the simmer time by 2 minutes to cook off the additional liquid.

Rayu

Chili Oil

One key element in traditional ramen is the finishing fat. It can be a slick of pork fat or a drizzle of blackened garlic oil, among many possibilities. My favorite one is rayu, a chili oil that is augmented with garlic, ginger, and scallion. It is easy to make and brings a nice zip to any bowl of ramen.

1 Tbsp minced or grated ginger (about 1 in [2.5 cm] length)

2 medium garlic cloves, minced

1 scallion, very thinly sliced

½ cup [120 ml] neutral oil, such as sunflower oil

¼ cup [30 g] red pepper flakes, preferably gochugaru (Korean red pepper flakes)

¼ cup [60 ml] toasted sesame oil

1 tsp MSG or ½ tsp kosher salt

In a small saucepan over low heat, combine the ginger, garlic, scallion, and neutral oil. Once the oil starts lightly bubbling, let cook and infuse, stirring occasionally, for 10 minutes. Add the red pepper flakes and infuse for 2 more minutes. Take the saucepan off the heat. Add the sesame oil and MSG and stir to combine.

Store in an airtight container in the refrigerator. As long as a sterile container was used, rayu can last for a long time. Once it's past 1 month, be sure to give it a sniff before using it.

TRY THIS   Add other spices, such as star anise, Sichuan peppercorns, or cumin. If needed, increase the amount of oil to accommodate the additional ingredients.

Focus the flavor by removing the aromatics and increasing the quantity of one or two ingredients. For example, for a garlic-scallion oil, remove the ginger and red pepper flakes, and triple the quantity of garlic and scallion used.

Ajitsuke Tamago

Jammy Egg

Ajitsuke tamago, also known as *ajitama*, is an iconic topping for traditional Japanese ramen. Eggs are soft-cooked and then marinated in a sweet soy liquid until the interior becomes bright orange and jammy. The ideal ajitama has a yolk that holds its shape and doesn't run into the soup.

During my testing, I realized that the jamminess of the yolk increases based on how long the egg marinates. As a result, the length of time you want to cook your egg depends on how long you plan to marinate it.

I find it frustrating when ajitama recipes don't include the volume of water used because this absolutely affects the cooking time. If you use too little water, the temperature drops considerably when you add the eggs, which means they cook less. I've included precise volumes so you can confidently make perfect eggs every time.

1 recipe (2 cups [475 ml]) Chashu Liquid (page 157)

3 qt [2.8 L] water

4 large eggs

Ice cubes

In a small saucepan, add the chashu liquid and bring to a simmer; simmer for 10 minutes.

In a medium pot, bring 2 quarts [1.9 L] of the water to a boil. Gently lower the eggs into the water and start a timer. While the eggs are cooking, put the remaining 1 quart [950 ml] of water into a large bowl and add ice cubes until the water reaches an ice-cold temperature.

If you plan on using the eggs within the next 24 hours, remove them from the boiling water after 7 minutes.

If you plan on letting the eggs marinate for at least 24 hours, remove them from the water after 6½ minutes.

If you plan on letting the eggs marinate for at least 48 hours, remove them from the water after 6 minutes and 15 seconds.

Transfer the eggs immediately to the ice water bath. Let them cool for 5 minutes. Peel the eggs and then put them in a container, covering them with the chashu liquid. Refrigerate for at least 1 hour before using. Use within 5 days.

TRY THIS Add other aromatics to the chashu liquid, such as star anise or cinnamon.

Soy-Caramel Mushrooms

This is not a traditional topping for ramen. It's my replacement for kikurage, seasoned wood ear mushrooms, which can be found in many ramen bowls in Japan. I have to admit that, while I love wood ear mushrooms, I've always found traditionally prepared kikurage to lack much flavor. This preparation brings together the earthiness of mushrooms with savory-sweet soy caramel—a combination I find delicious. As a bonus, it can be made with the humble button mushroom, which can be found everywhere.

8 oz [230 g] button mushrooms, sliced

1 Tbsp neutral oil, such as sunflower oil

1 Tbsp soy sauce

1 Tbsp sugar

Heat a 10 in [25 cm] skillet over medium-high heat. Add the mushrooms, dry, to the skillet (yes, without any oil!). They will release their water. Cook for about 6 minutes or until all the liquid has evaporated and the mushroom slices are starting to brown. Add the oil and sauté for 3 more minutes or until the mushroom slices are nicely browned. Decrease the heat to medium and add the soy sauce and sugar. Cook for 2 minutes, stirring constantly, or until the liquid has reduced and the mushrooms have taken on a deep brown color with a caramelly aroma. Add a splash of water and stir to release any caramel that has stuck to the pan.

TRY THIS   For more intense, complex flavors, use other varieties of mushrooms, such as oyster, trumpet, chanterelle, or shiitake.

Beyond Ramen

SOUPS

Egg Drop Ramen

With its gentle wisps of egg and sunny yellow chicken soup, this Cantonese dish is a familiar item on Chinese American restaurant menus across the country. I have a deep affection for this soup. During the winter, I love sipping on it, straight out of the container, as I walk the streets in New York City.

It's easy enough to make at home, and with the addition of instant ramen noodles, it becomes a meal in its own right. The turmeric is not absolutely necessary—it's in the recipe to give the soup a vivid yellow color.

2 cups [475 ml] water

One 3 to 3½ oz [85 to 100 g] packet instant ramen

1 Tbsp cornstarch

Generous pinch of ground turmeric (optional)

2 eggs, lightly beaten

1 scallion, very thinly sliced

PRE-SIMMER Add the water to a cold medium saucepan. Add the seasoning sachet, cornstarch, and turmeric, if using. Stir until the cornstarch has dissolved fully into the water. Turn the heat on to medium-high.

SIMMER Once the soup is simmering, add the noodle cake. Cook for 2 minutes or until your desired doneness. Note that it may take a little longer for the noodles to soften due to the cornstarch. Just before the noodles are done, using a fork or chopsticks, swirl the broth slowly and drizzle the egg in. It should form little ribbons as the soup swirls.

FINISH Pour the ramen into a bowl. Top with the scallion. Serve immediately.

TRY THIS Chinese American restaurants will typically serve crispy noodles with their egg drop soup. If there are any crunchy broken noodle pieces in the ramen package, save those and add them to each bite of soup.

For an Italian-style stracciatella soup, omit the turmeric and cornstarch, add 1 ounce [30 g] of grated Parmesan cheese to the eggs, and grate a touch of lemon zest into the soup. Top with more Parmesan cheese when you serve it.

Add aromatics, such as minced ginger or red pepper flakes, during the Simmer phase, or add a quick drizzle of sesame oil in the Finish phase.

Wonton Soup Ramen

Wonton in Cantonese can be roughly translated as "swallowing clouds," a lovely reference to how the little dumplings gently float around in this dish. The little packets of umami-rich meat and aromatics offer a pleasant contrast to the comforting, mild soup. If you opt to use premade dumplings, make sure you buy ones that are small enough to fit in a soupspoon.

One ¼ oz [7 g] packet powdered gelatin

2 cups [475 ml] low-sodium chicken stock or broth

2 scallions, chopped

1½ tsp minced or grated ginger (about ½ in [13 mm] length)

1 medium garlic clove, very thinly sliced

One 3 to 3½ oz [85 to 100 g] packet instant ramen

8 Basic Wontons (page 168)

Handful baby spinach

1 tsp sesame oil

1 tsp rice vinegar

PRE-SIMMER In a medium saucepan, add the gelatin and chicken stock and stir to combine. Let the gelatin bloom for at least 1 minute. Add the scallions, ginger, garlic, and seasoning sachet. Heat the saucepan over medium-high heat and stir again.

SIMMER Once the soup is simmering, add the wontons and cook for 1 minute. Add the noodle cake and cook for 2 minutes or until your desired doneness. However, 30 seconds before the noodles are done, add the baby spinach.

FINISH Take the saucepan off the heat. Stir in the sesame oil and rice vinegar. Pour into a bowl and serve immediately.

TRY THIS

To make a classic Korean holiday soup, add tteok (Korean rice cakes) in addition to the wontons at the Simmer phase.

To fortify the soup, swirl in a beaten egg at the Simmer phase.

Top the soup with leafy herbs, such as basil, parsley, cilantro, or mint, at the Finish phase.

Basic Wontons

4 oz [115 g] ground pork

½ tsp minced ginger

⅛ tsp freshly ground black pepper

1 Tbsp soy sauce

½ tsp sesame oil

½ tsp sugar

1 tsp mirin

1 tsp minced cilantro

One 14 oz [390 g] package square wonton wrappers

Add the pork, ginger, pepper, soy sauce, sesame oil, sugar, mirin, and cilantro to a medium bowl. Use your hands to thoroughly but gently mix the ingredients together, being careful not to compact the meat. Place a small bowl of water near your work surface. To assemble the wontons, place 1 teaspoon of filling in the center of a wrapper. Dip your finger into the water and run it along the edges of the wrapper. Fold the wonton so one corner touches the opposite corner and it forms a triangle. Press gently to push out any air and seal the edges.

Hold the triangle so it points away from you, with the filling nearer to you. Moisten one of the bottom corners. Bring the two bottom corners toward you and press them together to adhere. Repeat until you've used all the filling.

TRY THIS   Replace the pork with another ground protein, such as beef, chicken, turkey, or shrimp.

Replace the cilantro with other herbs, such as basil or chives.

Tomato and Egg Stir-Fry Ramen

You might be surprised to learn that a home-cooked favorite for many people across the broad expanse of China is a *tomato* dish. Tomatoes don't otherwise show up in most Chinese food, which makes the origins of this dish a mystery. (At least one author has posited that the dish was derived from Middle Eastern shakshuka.) However it got there, it's now considered a national comfort food staple. My version uses ketchup as a quick path to getting sweetness, umami, and brightness into the dish.

1 Tbsp neutral oil, such as sunflower oil

2 large eggs, beaten with a pinch of salt

1 cup [160 g] cherry tomatoes, halved (10 to 12 tomatoes)

2 cups [475 ml] water

2 Tbsp ketchup

One 3 to 3½ oz [85 to 100 g] packet instant ramen

PRE-SIMMER Heat a medium saucepan over medium high heat. Add the oil and swirl to coat the bottom of the pan.

Add the eggs and let them cook without stirring until the bottom sets, about 30 seconds. Using a fork, chopsticks, or a spatula, lift the edges of the egg and tilt the pan to let raw egg flow onto the bottom of the pan. Continue doing this until the egg is fully cooked and slightly browned, about 2 minutes total.

Break up the egg into large curds and add the tomatoes. Sauté the tomatoes for 2 minutes. And the water, ketchup, and seasoning sachet. Stir to combine.

SIMMER Once the soup is simmering, add the noodle cake and cook for 2 minutes or until your desired doneness.

FINISH Pour the ramen into a bowl. Arrange the tomatoes and eggs so some sit on top of the noodles. Serve immediately.

TRY THIS

When tomatoes are in season, replace cherry tomatoes with flavorful heirloom tomatoes, cut into cubes or slices.

One common addition is to drizzle 1 teaspoon of toasted sesame oil at the Finish phase.

Add thinly sliced scallions or herbs at the Finish phase for a fresh touch.

Pho Ramen
Vietnamese Beef Noodle Soup

Considered Vietnam's national dish, pho is thought to have developed during the French colonial period in the late nineteenth century, when the French introduced beef to the country. Vietnamese cooks likely used leftover beef bones to create hearty soups enlivened with warm spices such as star anise and cinnamon.

It's a dish that is difficult to reproduce at home due to the long cook time needed. Here I've done my best to create a recipe that can be made in minutes and captures the essential flavors of the dish. The recipe uses powdered gelatin to approximate the feel of a long-simmered soup. Traditionally, thinly shaved raw beef would be added, which requires special equipment or freezing and then slicing it. Good-quality deli roast beef actually works well and is much easier.

2 cups [475 ml] water

One ¼ oz [7 g] packet powdered gelatin

2 star anise pods

1 cinnamon stick

1 Tbsp neutral oil, such as sunflower oil

2 tsp sugar

1 tsp fish sauce

One 3 to 3½ oz [85 to 100 g] packet instant ramen

2 oz [55 g] thinly sliced deli roast beef

2 lime wedges

½ cup [50 g] mung bean sprouts

10 basil leaves

PRE-SIMMER In a medium saucepan, add the water and gelatin and stir to combine. Let the gelatin bloom for at least 1 minute. Add the star anise, cinnamon, oil, sugar, fish sauce, and seasoning sachet and stir again. Heat the saucepan over medium-high heat.

SIMMER Bring the soup to a simmer. Simmer for 2 minutes to let the flavors of the spices infuse into the soup, then add the noodle cake and cook for 2 minutes or until your desired doneness. Add the roast beef and heat for just a few seconds to warm it up.

FINISH Take the saucepan off the heat. Squeeze in the juice of 1 lime wedge. Pour the ramen into a bowl. Top with the remaining lime wedge, the bean sprouts, and basil leaves. Serve immediately.

TRY THIS For a vegetarian version, omit the gelatin, use soy-flavored instant ramen, replace the fish sauce with soy sauce, and replace the beef with prepared tofu or another vegetarian protein.

Add other leafy herbs, such as cilantro or mint.

For some fieriness, add thinly sliced jalapeños and a drizzle of sriracha at the Finish phase.

Soupe au Pistou Ramen

French Vegetable and Bean Soup

In Provence, in the southeast of France, it's common to cook with a pesto-like sauce called *pistou*. The one major difference from its Italian cousin is that pistou does not have pine nuts. Fortunately, they are similar enough that they can be used interchangeably. In soupe au pistou, the condiment enriches a hearty vegetable and bean soup. I'm sure grandmothers in Provence would faint at the idea of making this traditional soup with instant ramen and frozen vegetables. But I'm convinced if they took a bite, they'd change their minds right away.

¾ cup [120 g] canned cannellini beans, drained

1 Tbsp tomato paste

2 cups [475 ml] water

3 sprigs thyme or 1½ tsp dried thyme leaves

1 cup [140 g] frozen mixed vegetables, preferably Mediterranean

One 3 to 3½ oz [85 to 100 g] packet instant ramen, noodles broken into small pieces

1 Tbsp extra-virgin olive oil

1 Tbsp pesto, jarred or homemade (see page 117)

PRE-SIMMER Put ¼ cup [40 g] of the beans into a medium saucepan and mash them with a fork to form a paste. Add the tomato paste and water and stir to combine. Add the thyme, frozen vegetables, and seasoning sachet. Turn the heat up to medium-high.

SIMMER Once the soup is simmering, let it cook for 2 minutes, then add the noodle cake. Cook for 2 minutes or until your desired doneness.

FINISH Pour the ramen into a bowl. Drizzle the olive oil over the top and add the pesto as a dollop in the middle of the soup. Serve immediately.

TRY THIS

For a vegetarian version, use soy-flavored instant ramen.

Use any mix of diced vegetables that are in season. If you use any vegetables that require a longer cook time, such as potatoes, eggplant, or celery, increase the Simmer time accordingly.

For a soupier version, use half of the noodle cake and increase the water to 2½ cups [600 ml].

Naengmyeon Ramen

Korean Cold Noodle Soup

The Korean summer dish of choice is naengmyeon, which literally means "cold noodle." It's not just served cold—it's served *ice-cold*. The secret ingredient here is lemon-lime soda, a trick that is used by many Koreans in recipes that call for a sweet broth or marinade.

Normally, naengmyeon is made with chewy buckwheat noodles. While instant ramen noodles have a different texture, this recipe does a surprisingly good job at approximating the flavors of this beloved dish.

¾ cup [180 ml] lemon-lime soda, such as Sprite or 7UP

2¾ cups [655 ml] water

1 Tbsp rice vinegar

1 tsp soy sauce

One 3 to 3½ oz [85 to 100 g] packet instant ramen

¼ daikon, thinly sliced and quartered

¼ cucumber, julienned

¼ apple, thinly sliced (preferably a crisp variety, such as Fuji)

1 hard-boiled egg or Ajitsuke Tamago (Jammy Egg, page 160), sliced in half lengthwise

½ scallion, thinly sliced

Dijon mustard

Toasted sesame seeds

PRE-SIMMER In a medium bowl, combine the soda, ¾ cup [180 ml] of the water, the rice vinegar, and soy sauce. Add the seasoning sachet and stir to combine.

SIMMER In a medium saucepan, bring the remaining 2 cups [475 ml] of water to a simmer over medium-high heat. Cook the noodle cake for 2½ minutes or until your desired doneness. Drain the noodles and rinse them with water until they have cooled down.

FINISH Add a handful of ice cubes to the bowl with the soda mixture—enough for the broth to become ice-cold. Place the noodles in the middle of the bowl. Top with the daikon, cucumber, apple, egg, and scallion. Add a dollop of mustard and sprinkle sesame seeds on top. Serve immediately.

TRY THIS To make a vegetarian version, use a soy-flavored instant ramen.

For a spicier, funkier version, top with kimchi. Add some of the kimchi pickling liquid to the broth.

For added brightness, sprinkle rice vinegar on the cucumber and radish pieces before adding them to the bowl.

AIR DRIED 생면

Enlarged to show texture
Serving Suggestion
Présentation suggérée
조리예

STEWS

Frijoles de la Olla Ramen

Mexican Stewed Beans

RECOMMENDED RAMEN: Soy-Flavored Classic

Traditionally, this Mexican staple is simmered for hours in an olla, or clay pot. It turns out you can achieve a similar result by using canned beans and fortifying them with some fat, onion, garlic, and oregano. This dish is an excellent canvas for a wide range of garnishes, allowing you to take it in numerous directions based on whatever you have on hand.

1 Tbsp lard or extra-virgin olive oil

⅓ cup [45 g] diced onion (about ⅛ large onion)

1 medium garlic clove, very thinly sliced

¾ cup [110 g] drained canned pinto or black beans

Pinch of dried oregano

One 3 to 3½ oz [85 to 100 g] packet instant ramen

1 cup [240 ml] water

Cilantro, chopped, for garnish (optional)

Radishes, thinly sliced, for garnish (optional)

Cotija cheese, for garnish (optional)

Jalapeño, sliced, for garnish (optional)

Tomato, diced, for garnish (optional)

Lime wedges, for garnish (optional)

PRE-SIMMER Heat a medium saucepan over medium-high heat. Add the lard and onion. Sauté the onion until it has caramelized, about 4 minutes. Add the garlic and sauté for 15 seconds or until fragrant but not browned. Add the beans, oregano, seasoning sachet, and water.

SIMMER Bring the soup to a simmer. Add the noodle cake and cook for 2 minutes or until your desired doneness.

FINISH Pour the ramen into a bowl. If you're adding garnishes, top the ramen with cilantro, radishes, cotija cheese, jalapeño, and tomato. Serve immediately with lime wedges.

TRY THIS For a more Tex-Mex flavor, add 1 teaspoon of cumin (whole or ground) with the garlic.

Try other garnishes, such as corn kernels (canned or fresh), crumbled tortilla chips, sliced avocado, and sliced scallions.

Ajiáco Ramen
Colombian Potato Stew

Ask any homesick Colombian from Bogotá what they want to eat, and their likely response is, "¡Ajiáco!" This bountiful stew is an homage to the region's deep connections to the potato and comes with an array of toppings, including a segment of a whole corncob. This recipe is a simplification of the traditional version, which uses a variety of different potatoes, including one that breaks down and enriches the soup. Instead, I use potato flakes to thicken things up—it works quite well.

Guasca is an important herb in Colombian cuisine. You can find it online and in Latin groceries. Some people find that oregano is an acceptable substitute, but I disagree. If you don't have it, I don't recommend trying to use a substitute herb—the stew will still be delicious.

---

2 cups [475 ml] low-sodium chicken stock or broth

⅓ whole corncob or ¼ cup [35 g] corn kernels

5 fingerling potatoes, cut into ⅜ in [1 cm] thick rounds (about 1 cup [140 g])

2 Tbsp dried guascas (optional, see headnote)

One 3 to 3½ oz [85 to 100 g] packet instant ramen

Salt

⅓ cup [20 g] dried potato flakes

3 oz [85 g] rotisserie chicken breast, shredded

¼ avocado, sliced

3 sprigs cilantro, chopped

1 Tbsp heavy cream

1 tsp capers

PRE-SIMMER Add the stock, corncob, potatoes, guascas (if using), and seasoning sachet to a medium saucepan. Turn the heat to high. Add a generous pinch of salt.

SIMMER Bring the soup to a simmer and decrease the heat to medium. Simmer for 3 minutes. Add the noodle cake and cook for 2 minutes or until your desired doneness. Add the potato flakes and stir until incorporated into the soup.

FINISH Pour the ramen into a wide bowl. Top with the chicken, avocado, cilantro, cream, and capers. Serve immediately.

TRY THIS

If you don't have a rotisserie chicken handy, you can add 1 chicken thigh, thinly sliced, to the saucepan along with the corncob and potatoes. Add a generous pinch of salt.

A squeeze of lime or lemon juice brings welcome brightness.

Use different toppings at the Finish stage, including chili oil, different herbs, sliced sausage, and shredded cheese.

Moqueca Ramen
Brazilian Seafood Stew

This recipe is halfway between a moqueca baiana (from Bahia in the northeast of Brazil) and a moqueca capixaba (from Espirito Santo, in the southeast of Brazil). The former uses coconut milk and dende oil, or red palm oil, while the latter forgoes coconut milk and uses olive oil. I like the creaminess that the coconut milk brings, and I use olive oil because it's difficult to find good dende oil in the United States. Between the rich broth, fish, and shrimp, this is a hefty, soul-satisfying dish to make. This recipe serves two people. If the fish fillet is thicker than ½ inch [13 mm], then it should be sliced.

1 Tbsp extra-virgin olive oil

½ red bell pepper, very thinly sliced

1 medium garlic clove, very thinly sliced

1 Tbsp tomato paste

1 cup [240 ml] coconut milk

½ cup [120 ml] water

1 tsp fish sauce

5 sprigs cilantro, chopped

One 3 to 3½ oz [85 to 100 g] packet instant ramen

3 oz [85 g] frozen ½ in [13 mm] thick whitefish fillet, such as tilapia, cod, or mahi mahi

3 oz [85 g] frozen shrimp (about six 31/40 shrimp)

¼ lime, plus an additional slice for garnish

PRE-SIMMER Heat a medium saucepan over medium-high heat. Add the oil and bell pepper. Sauté for 2 minutes or until the pepper has softened a little. Add the garlic and tomato paste and cook for 30 seconds or until fragrant but not burned. Add the coconut milk, water, fish sauce, cilantro, and seasoning sachet. Stir to combine.

SIMMER Bring the soup to a simmer. Add the fish and simmer for 1 minute. Add the shrimp and noodle cake. Cook for 2 minutes or until your desired doneness. Give the fish and shrimp a poke to check if they are fully cooked.

FINISH Squeeze in the juice of the ¼ lime and stir. Pour the ramen into a large bowl, arranging the fish and shrimp so they are visible. Garnish with an additional slice of lime and serve immediately.

TRY THIS Replace the shrimp and/or fish with other seafood, such as mussels, scallops, or clams. Adjust the cooking time to ensure whatever you add is fully cooked.

For a fiery kick, add thinly sliced chile along with the bell pepper slices.

Fasolia Ramen
Middle Eastern Green Bean Stew

Fasolia is a staple dish of stewed beans found across the Middle East. This recipe is inspired by a version from Palestine, Syria, and Jordan that uses green beans.

Traditionally, fasolia would be cooked for an extended period of time until the green beans are meltingly tender. Here, I recommend using frozen green beans. They still have excellent flavor and texture, and they cook quickly enough that you can achieve tenderness in just a few minutes. It doesn't quite reach the softness of the simmered-all-afternoon stuff, but it'll still hit the spot.

1 Tbsp extra-virgin olive oil

2 garlic cloves, very thinly sliced

¼ tsp allspice

2 Tbsp tomato paste

One 3 to 3½ oz [85 to 100 g] packet instant ramen

1½ cups [210 g] frozen, cut green beans

1½ cups [360 ml] water

Parsley, chopped, for garnish (optional)

PRE-SIMMER Heat a saucepan over medium heat. Add the oil and garlic. Gently cook the garlic for 30 seconds, taking care not to brown the garlic. Add the allspice and let it bloom for 15 seconds or until fragrant. Add the tomato paste, seasoning sachet, green beans, and water.

SIMMER Once the soup is simmering, cook for 2 minutes. Add the noodle cake and cook for 2 minutes or until your desired doneness.

FINISH Pour the ramen into a bowl and garnish with the parsley, if using. Serve immediately.

TRY THIS For a vegetarian version, use soy-flavored instant ramen.

For a meaty version, sear 4 ounces [115 g] of ground beef during the Pre-Simmer phase and decrease the green beans to 1 cup [140 g].

Replace ½ cup [70 g] of green beans with another vegetable, such as carrots, cut in a small dice.

Shakshuka Ramen

Tomato and Pepper Stew with Eggs

You might be familiar with shakshuka as a brunch favorite from North Africa and the Middle East. It turns out that it's a dish that exists under different names in cultures around the Mediterranean Sea, including in Spain (huevos a la flamenca), Italy (uovos in purgatorio), and Greece (avga me domates).

They can't all be wrong. And indeed, there's something deeply satisfying about the combination of eggs with a savory-tart vegetable stew. With the addition of instant ramen noodles, it works as a standalone dish. My version takes a cue from Middle Eastern flavors thanks to the cumin and paprika. This dish serves two.

2 Tbsp extra-virgin olive oil

½ cup [70 g] thinly sliced onion (about ¼ large onion)

½ cup [60 g] thinly sliced red bell pepper (about ½ medium bell pepper)

1 medium garlic clove, very thinly sliced

One 3½ to 4½ oz [100 to 125 g] packet instant ramen, noodle cake broken into chunks

½ tsp whole or ground cumin

2 tsp paprika

1 cup [240 g] canned crushed or ground tomatoes

1 cup [240 ml] water

4 large eggs

Salt

¼ cup [30 g] crumbled feta

Parsley leaves, for garnish (optional)

PRE-SIMMER Heat the oil in a 10-inch [25 cm] skillet over medium-high heat. Add the onion, bell pepper, garlic, and seasoning sachet. Sauté for 4 minutes or until the onion and bell pepper have softened. Add the cumin and paprika and cook for 30 seconds. Add the tomatoes and water and stir to combine. Add the noodle chunks in an *X* pattern in the skillet, ensuring they are at least partially submerged. Crack the eggs into the four empty spots left by that pattern. Add a pinch of salt to each egg.

SIMMER Bring the stew to a simmer and cover. Cook for 3 minutes or until the eggs have reached your desired doneness.

FINISH Sprinkle the feta and parsley, if using, on top of the stew. Serve immediately directly out of the pan.

TRY THIS Sauté a couple of links of sliced sausage, such as merguez sausage, with the peppers and onions.

Replace the onions or peppers with chickpeas or other vegetables, such as peas or thinly sliced leeks.

Dollop yogurt, sour cream, or labneh on top at the Finish phase to give the dish some creaminess.

Couscous Ramen

This staple dish found across North Africa is typically composed of small pellets of semolina served with a meat and vegetable stew spiked with garlic, ginger, and turmeric. While a traditional meat couscous can take hours to reach the proper fork-tender texture, a vegetable one can be made in minutes with the help of instant ramen. To approximate the semolina pellets, I break up the noodle cake finely and hydrate the noodle bits with just a little boiling water. Aside from this recipe concept, you can use this technique anytime you want to have a couscous-like presentation of the noodles to serve alongside a stew or soup.

One 3 to 3½ oz [85 to 100 g] packet instant ramen, noodles crushed into small pieces

½ cup [120 ml] boiling water

2 Tbsp extra-virgin olive oil

½ medium carrot, cut into sticks 3 in [7.5 cm] long by ¼ in [6 mm] wide

½ cup [70 g] diced onion (about ¼ large onion)

1 Tbsp minced or grated ginger (about 1 in [2.5 cm] length)

1 medium garlic clove, very thinly sliced

¾ cup [180 ml] water

½ cup [120 g] canned crushed or ground tomatoes

¼ tsp ground turmeric

½ small zucchini, cut into sticks 3 in [7.5 cm] long by ¼ in [6 mm] wide

½ cup [80 g] chickpeas

PRE-SIMMER Add the noodle bits to a small container. Pour the boiling water over the noodles and cover. After 3 minutes, add 1 tablespoon of the olive oil and stir.

Heat the remaining 1 tablespoon of olive oil in a medium saucepan over medium-high heat. Add the carrot, onion, ginger, garlic, and seasoning sachet. Sauté for 2 minutes or until the vegetables have softened. Add the ¾ cup [180 ml] of water.

SIMMER Bring the stew to a simmer and cook for 3 minutes. Add the crushed tomatoes, turmeric, zucchini, and chickpeas. Simmer for 3 more minutes.

FINISH Put the noodles into a wide bowl. Pour the stew over the ramen. If desired, arrange the zucchini and carrot sticks in an alternating pattern around the top of the stew as pictured. Serve immediately.

TRY THIS Replace the carrots or zucchini with other vegetables cut into sticks. Other classic couscous vegetables include turnips, cabbage, sweet potatoes, and pumpkin or winter squash such as butternut.

Add other North African spices, such as saffron, cinnamon, cumin, or ras el hanout.

For a sweet note, add raisins, prunes, or dried apricots at the beginning of the Simmer phase.

Mafe Ramen
West African Peanut Stew

I served in the Peace Corps in Cameroon, where I regularly ate sauce d'arachide, a rich, deeply nourishing stew with a thick texture from ground peanuts. I have fond memories of dipping fufu (a pounded starch dish) into the stew and licking it off my fingers. It turns out that variations of this dish can be found across West Africa. In some countries, including Senegal and Mali, it's known as *mafe* (pronounced MAH-fay). Wherever it's gone, it's become a beloved staple dish, and for good reason—as you'll find out if you try this recipe.

1 tsp neutral oil, such as sunflower oil

4 oz [115 g] ground beef, preferably 80/20

½ cup [40 g] diced cabbage

1 medium garlic clove, minced

1 Tbsp minced or grated ginger (about 1 in [2.5 cm] length)

2 Tbsp tomato paste

1½ cups [360 ml] water

2 Tbsp peanut butter

1 Scotch bonnet or habanero chile (optional)

One 3 to 3½ oz [85 to 100 g] packet instant ramen

PRE-SIMMER Heat a medium saucepan over high heat. Add the oil, beef, and cabbage. Sear for 3 minutes or until the beef and cabbage have browned. Lower the heat to medium, add the garlic and ginger, and let them bloom for 30 seconds or until fragrant. Add the tomato paste and cook for 15 to 30 seconds or until fragrant. Add the water, peanut butter, Scotch bonnet chile, if using, and seasoning sachet. Scrape up any browned bits stuck to the pan and stir to incorporate the peanut butter into the soup.

SIMMER Bring the soup to a simmer. Add the noodle cake and cook for 2 minutes or until your desired doneness.

FINISH Pour the ramen into a bowl. Serve immediately. If you added a Scotch bonnet pepper, you can discard it or, if you're feeling brave, nibble on it as you eat the dish.

TRY THIS Add ½ cup [70 g] of diced stew vegetables, such as sweet potatoes, carrots, or potatoes.

For a seafood version of this dish, replace the beef with one small fillet (about 4 ounces [115 g]) from a whitefish such as tilapia or mahi mahi.

Add the fish at the Simmer phase and let it simmer for 1 minute before adding the noodle cake.

Beef Stroganoff Ramen

This traditional dish of beef, sour cream, and mustard may have originated in Russia, but it has now become a global comfort dish, with numerous regional variations. Americans eat it with egg noodles, the Japanese eat it with white rice, and Brazilians top it with crispy shoestring potatoes. It's about time for a version with instant ramen noodles, don't you think?

4 oz [115 g] ground beef, preferably 80/20

4 white mushrooms, thinly sliced

½ cup [70 g] diced onion (about ¼ large onion)

1 tsp Dijon mustard

One 3 to 3½ oz [85 to 100 g] packet instant ramen

1½ cups [360 ml] water

¼ cup [60 g] sour cream

½ scallion, thinly sliced

Black pepper

PRE-SIMMER Heat a medium saucepan over high heat. Add the beef, mushrooms, and onion. Sear the ingredients for 5 minutes, turning periodically, or until the beef has browned and the mushrooms and onion have lost their moisture. Add the mustard, seasoning sachet, and water.

SIMMER Decrease the heat to medium-high and bring the soup to a simmer. Add the noodle cake and cook for 2 minutes or until your desired doneness.

FINISH Take the saucepan off the heat. Stir in the sour cream until incorporated into the soup. Pour the ramen into a bowl and top with the scallion and black pepper. Serve immediately.

TRY THIS Use different herbs to finish the dish, such as parsley, tarragon, or sage.

Use different varieties of mushrooms, such as meaty shiitakes or earthy porcinis.

Borscht Ramen

Earthy beets, rich pork fat, aromatic dill, smooth sour cream—borscht brings together a lovely array of flavors that work surprisingly well as a noodle soup. While the dish can be found across Eastern Europe and Russia, this version is inspired by Ukrainian borscht. Traditionally, whole cuts of beef or pork would be used. To speed things along, I use bacon, which renders its fat quickly and adds a smoky note.

2 slices bacon, cut into 1 in [2.5 cm] pieces

½ medium beet, shredded (about ¾ cup [45 g])

¼ cup [20 g] shredded cabbage

2 cups [475 ml] water

1 Tbsp tomato paste

One 3 to 3½ oz [85 to 100 g] packet instant ramen

1 Tbsp sour cream, for serving

Dill fronds, for garnish

PRE-SIMMER Add the bacon, beet, and cabbage to a cold medium saucepan. Heat the saucepan over medium-high heat. Once the bacon starts sizzling, sauté the ingredients for 3 minutes or until the bacon has rendered some of its fat and has browned. Add the water, tomato paste, and seasoning sachet. Stir to incorporate the tomato paste into the soup.

SIMMER Bring the soup to a simmer and then let it cook for 6 minutes. Add the noodle cake and cook for 2 minutes or until your desired doneness.

FINISH Pour the ramen into a bowl. Top with the sour cream and garnish with dill. Serve immediately.

TRY THIS   For a vegetarian version, replace the bacon with 1 tablespoon of neutral oil and crumbled seitan, and use soy-flavored instant ramen.

For additional acidity, add 1 teaspoon of apple cider or red wine vinegar during the Simmer phase.

Replace some beet or cabbage with thinly sliced potatoes.

Aloo Gobi Ramen
South Asian Cauliflower and Potato Stew

Aloo gobi literally means "potato cauliflower," which gives you a clear sense of the main ingredients of this dish, one of the most popular vegetable stews in South Asia. Beyond those two components, each recipe seems to have its own signature bouquet of spices and aromatics. In my version, I find the addition of garam masala to be intoxicating with its fragrant warm spice notes.

1 Tbsp unsalted butter

1 Tbsp minced or grated ginger (about 1 in [2.5 cm] length)

1 medium garlic clove, minced

½ tsp ground cumin

¼ tsp red pepper flakes

1 Tbsp tomato paste

¼ tsp ground turmeric

¼ tsp garam masala

2 cups [475 ml] water

One 3 to 3½ oz [85 to 100 g] packet instant ramen

1 medium Yukon gold potato, thinly sliced into half-moons

1 cup [140 g] cauliflower florets

Salt

Cilantro leaves, for garnish (optional)

PRE-SIMMER Heat a medium saucepan over medium heat. Add the butter. Once the butter has melted and started to foam, add the ginger, garlic, cumin, and red pepper flakes, letting them bloom for 30 seconds or until fragrant. Add the tomato paste, turmeric, and garam masala. Cook the tomato paste for 15 to 30 seconds or until lightly browned. Increase the heat to medium-high. Add the water, seasoning sachet, potato, cauliflower, and a generous pinch of salt.

SIMMER Bring the soup to a simmer. Cook the vegetables for 3 minutes, then add the noodle cake. Cook for 2 minutes or until your desired doneness.

FINISH Pour the ramen into a bowl. Garnish with cilantro, if using. Serve immediately.

TRY THIS Use different quantities of spices and add others into the mix, such as ground coriander and curry powder.

Use other vegetables, such as peas or broccoli. You can think of this recipe as a good template for a vegetable stew with South Asian flavors.

For a brighter dish, squeeze lemon or lime juice on in the Finish phase.

Thai Green Curry Ramen

One of the anchors of Thai cuisine is its array of aromatic curries, many of which are built on top of flavorful pastes. The good news is that you can purchase good-quality curry pastes that make it possible to produce an excellent Thai curry at home. Of all the colors of curry, green is the fieriest because it uses fresh green chiles (whereas red curry paste uses milder dried red chiles). Note that canned bamboo shoot quality varies widely. If you open the can and there is a strong, unpleasant smell, leave it out. I've found La Choy brand canned bamboo shoots to be reliable.

1 Tbsp neutral oil, such as sunflower oil

4 oz [115 g] boneless, skinless chicken thigh (about 1 thigh), cut into ½ in [13 mm] thick slices

1½ cups [360 ml] water

½ cup [120 ml] coconut milk

1 cup [80 g] quartered and thinly sliced eggplant

1 oz [30 g] canned bamboo shoots, preferably La Choy brand, drained and rinsed

2 Tbsp Thai green curry paste (I recommend Maesri or Aroy-D brands)

1 tsp sugar

1 tsp fish sauce

10 basil leaves, plus more for garnish

One 3 to 3½ oz [85 to 100 g] packet instant ramen

PRE-SIMMER Heat a medium saucepan over high heat. Add the oil and chicken. Sear for 3 minutes or until the chicken has browned. Add the water, coconut milk, eggplant, bamboo shoots, curry paste, sugar, fish sauce, basil leaves, and half of the seasoning sachet. Lower the heat to medium-high.

SIMMER Once the soup is simmering, let it cook for 3 minutes. Add the noodle cake and cook for 2 minutes or until your desired doneness.

FINISH Pour the ramen into a bowl and arrange the ingredients so they are all visible. Top with additional basil leaves for garnish. Serve immediately.

TRY THIS For a vegetarian version, use a soy-flavored instant ramen and replace the chicken thigh with tofu. Replace the fish sauce with soy sauce.

For a pop of color, replace some of the eggplant with thinly sliced red bell pepper.

Add other herbs, such as cilantro and mint, to bring forward herbal flavors. For intense spiciness, add thinly sliced Thai bird chiles at the Finish phase.

Coconut Chicken Ramen

Unlike many of the other recipes in this book, this one is not related to a specific traditional dish, though it is generally inspired by Thai flavors. It's a dish I make when I'm in need of a restorative, calming bowl of noodle soup. The garlic-, ginger-, and chicken-infused soup, enriched with coconut milk, brings comfort, while the ample green vegetables give a feeling of healthful nourishment.

1 Tbsp neutral oil, such as sunflower oil

4 oz [115 g] boneless, skinless chicken thigh (about 1 thigh), cut into ½ in [13 mm] chunks

1 garlic clove, very thinly sliced

1 Tbsp minced or grated ginger (about 1 in [2.5 cm] length)

1½ cups [360 ml] water

½ cup [120 ml] coconut milk

½ tsp ground turmeric

One 3 to 3½ oz [85 to 100 g] packet instant ramen

1 cup [70 g] broccoli florets

Handful baby spinach

4 sprigs cilantro, leaves plucked and stems chopped, for garnish

Red pepper flakes (optional)

PRE-SIMMER Heat the oil in a medium saucepan over high heat. Sear the chicken for 3 minutes or until browned all over. Lower the heat to medium. Add the garlic and ginger, blooming them for 30 seconds or until fragrant. Add the water, coconut milk, turmeric, seasoning sachet, and broccoli. Scrape up any browned bits stuck to the saucepan.

SIMMER Bring the soup to a simmer. Cook for 1 minute, then add the noodle cake and cook for 2 minutes or until your desired doneness. However, 30 seconds before your noodles are done, add the spinach to the soup.

FINISH Pour the ramen into a bowl. Garnish with cilantro and, if using, a dusting of red pepper flakes. Serve immediately.

TRY THIS Replace the broccoli with other vegetables, such as cauliflower, red bell pepper, or whatever happens to be in season. Replace the baby spinach with other leafy greens or herbs.

Replace the chicken with other proteins, such as ground beef or tofu.

Add some brightness with lime juice or rice vinegar.

Budae Jjigae

Korean Army Stew

During and after the Korean War, impoverished Koreans repurposed US military rations to create this stew. As the child of two Korean immigrants who survived the war, this dish is quite meaningful. To me, it represents the culture's resilience in the face of hardship. This is one of the few ramen recipes in this book that serves two. It's difficult to imagine creating a single-serving version of budae jjigae—it is, by design, a bountiful meal.

One 4½ oz [125 g] packet instant ramen

1 Tbsp gochujang

3 cups [710 ml] water

6 oz [170 g] SPAM, sliced

2 oz [55 g] enoki or button mushrooms, sliced

5 oz [140 g] tofu (about one-third of a 14 oz [400 g] block), sliced

½ cup [75 g] sliced kimchi

1 hot dog, sliced

15 oval tteok (Korean rice cakes)

1 slice American cheese

1 scallion, thinly sliced

PRE-SIMMER Add the seasoning sachet, dried vegetable sachet, gochujang, and water to a large bowl. Stir to combine.

In a 10- to 11-inch [25 to 27.5 cm] wide pot, starting at 12 o'clock and going clockwise around the pot, add the SPAM, mushrooms, tofu, kimchi, hot dog, and rice cakes. Leave an open space in the middle for the noodle cake. Gently pour the liquid over all the ingredients without disturbing their placement.

SIMMER Turn the heat up to medium-high and bring to a simmer. Nestle the noodle cake into the center of the pot. Gently jiggle the noodle cake to help it cook, taking care not to break up the overall shape of the noodle cake. Cook for 4 minutes or to your desired doneness.

FINISH Bring the pot to the table. Top with the American cheese and scallion. Ladle the stew into individual serving bowls and serve immediately.

TRY THIS   For an even more nourishing stew, add ¼ cup [35 g] of canned baked beans (or any canned beans) during the Pre-Simmer phase and/or crack 2 eggs into the soup while simmering.

Replace the hot dog and/or SPAM with other sliced sausages and meats, such as Italian sausage, kielbasa, breakfast sausage, or bacon.

RECOMMENDED
RAMEN:
Spicy Korean
style

Kimchi Jjigae Ramen

Korean Kimchi Stew

This fiery stew, acidic and pungent from the kimchi and enrobed in pork fat, is near to my heart. It's one of my mom's and my favorite Korean dishes—and I always make it for her when she comes to visit. It's a stew that tastes like home. I like adding brine from the kimchi jar at the end. It brings more zip and funk from the raw garlic and cabbage, as well as a dose of probiotics.

2 slices bacon, sliced

½ cup [40 g] diced cabbage

2 cups [475 ml] water

One 4½ oz [125 g] packet Instant ramen

½ cup [75 g] sliced kimchi

3½ oz [100 g] firm or extra-firm tofu (about one-quarter of a 14 oz [400 g] block), cubed

Kimchi pickling liquid

½ scallion, very thinly sliced

PRE-SIMMER Add the bacon and cabbage to a cold medium saucepan. Heat the saucepan over medium-high heat. Once the bacon start sizzling, cook for 3 minutes or until the fat has rendered out of the bacon and the bacon and cabbage have browned. Add the water, half of the seasoning sachet, and the kimchi.

SIMMER Once the soup is simmering, let it cook for 2 minutes. Add the noodle cake and tofu and cook for 2 minutes or until your desired doneness.

FINISH Pour the ramen into a bowl, add a splash of kimchi liquid, and garnish with the scallions. Serve immediately.

TRY THIS   Add an extra ½ cup [70 g] of chopped vegetables, such as mushrooms, daikon radish, or broccoli, at the Simmer phase.

Crack an egg into the soup along with the noodle cake at the Simmer phase.

Tantanmen

Japanese Sesame, Pork, and Chili Ramen

Tantanmen, a popular style of ramen in Japan, has a rich sesame broth laced with fatty pork and chili oil. It is a descendent of Sichuanese dan dan noodles, a dish that has a similar fiery flavor profile. My instant ramen adaptation is satisfying because it covers a lot of flavor bases: meaty, savory, nutty, fiery, vegetal, pungent, fatty, *and* acidic.

4 oz [115 g] ground pork

2 cups [475 ml] water

2 Tbsp tahini

1 tsp miso

1 Tbsp rice vinegar

One 4½ oz [125 g] packet instant ramen

2 bok choy leaves

1 scallion, thinly sliced

Toasted sesame seeds, for garnish

Rayu (chili oil, page 159) or chili crisp (optional)

PRE-SIMMER Heat a medium saucepan over high heat. Sear the pork for 3 minutes or until browned.

Add the water to the saucepan and scrape up any pork that's stuck to the pan. Add the tahini, miso, rice vinegar, and seasoning sachet. Stir to combine. Decrease the heat to medium-high.

SIMMER Bring the soup to a simmer, add the noodle cake, and cook for 3 minutes or until your desired doneness. With 30 seconds remaining for your desired cook time, add the bok choy to the simmering saucepan. You're giving the bok choy just a brief dip in hot water. I find that it gets unpleasantly chewy if cooked longer than that.

FINISH Pour into a bowl. Arrange the bok choy to one side of the bowl. Garnish with the scallion, sesame seeds, and rayu, if using. Serve immediately.

TRY THIS   For a vegetarian version, use a soy-flavored ramen and replace the pork with ground seitan, seared in 1 tablespoon of neutral oil such as sunflower oil. Add red pepper flakes.

Don't have tahini? Replace it with peanut butter or any other nut butter.

Substitute other greens for the bok choy, such as mustard greens, mizuna, or spinach. Pickles such as kimchi are a nice addition to counter-balance the heaviness of the soup.

Mapo Tofu Ramen

Sichuanese Fiery and Tingly Tofu Stew

RECOMMENDED RAMEN:
Beef-Flavored
Classic

This oil-slicked stew from China's Sichuan province is one you don't just taste but also *feel*. Mapo tofu perfectly embodies the Sichuanese flavor concept of mala: the combination of fiery heat from chiles and buzzing from Sichuan peppercorns.

It's typically made with doubanjiang, a Chinese fermented chili bean paste that is unfortunately not commonly available in supermarkets. I find that the combination of miso and chili crisp is a good substitute for this ingredient.

2 oz [55 g] ground pork or beef

1 tsp ground Sichuan peppercorns

2 cups [475 ml] water

2 tsp miso

One 3 to 3½ oz [85 to 100 g] packet instant ramen

6 oz [170 g] silken tofu (half a 12 oz [340 g] package)

2 Tbsp chili crisp

½ scallion, thinly sliced, for garnish

PRE-SIMMER Heat a medium saucepan over high heat. Sear the ground meat for 3 minutes or until it has browned. Lower the heat to medium. Add the Sichuan peppercorns and let them bloom for 15 seconds or until fragrant. Add the water, miso, and seasoning sachet.

SIMMER Bring the soup to a simmer. Add the noodle cake and silken tofu. Cook, breaking up the silken tofu with a spoon, for 2 minutes or until your desired doneness.

FINISH Add the chili crisp and stir to incorporate it into the soup. Pour the ramen into a bowl and top with the scallion. Serve immediately.

TRY THIS For a vegetarian version, use a soy-flavored instant ramen and replace the meat with ground seitan.

For an additional savory note, try adding sliced mushrooms with the ground meat.

Xi'an-Style Cumin Lamb Ramen

RECOMMENDED
RAMEN:
Beef-Flavored
Classic

I first came across this dish at Xi'an Famous Foods in Flushing, Queens, a restaurant that serves food from Western China. I found the flavor combination of spices, herbs, and chile on their thick, hand-pulled noodles to be nothing short of intoxicating. I wasn't the only one, apparently—the restaurant has received national recognition for this and other dishes. This is my instant ramen homage to the harmony of flavors in their cumin lamb dish.

One ¼ oz [7 g] packet powdered gelatin

2 cups [475 ml] water

4 oz [115 g] ground lamb

1½ tsp ground cumin

½ tsp ground Sichuan peppercorns

2 Tbsp chili crisp or Rayu (chili oil, page 159)

½ cup [60 g] diced celery

½ cup [40 g] diced cabbage

2 tsp rice vinegar

One 3 to 3½ oz [85 to 100 g] packet instant ramen

4 sprigs cilantro, leaves removed and stems chopped, for garnish

PRE-SIMMER In a measuring cup or bowl, add the gelatin to the water and stir to combine. Let the gelatin bloom for at least 1 minute.

Heat a medium saucepan over high heat. Sear the lamb for 3 minutes or until browned. Lower the heat to medium. Add the cumin, Sichuan peppercorns, chili crisp, celery, and cabbage. Sauté for 2 minutes. Add the gelatin water, vinegar, and seasoning sachet to the saucepan.

SIMMER Once the soup is simmering, cook for 2 minutes. Add the noodle cake and cook for 2 minutes or until your desired doneness.

FINISH Pour the ramen into a bowl and garnish with the cilantro. Serve immediately.

TRY THIS For a vegetarian version, omit the gelatin, use a soy-flavored instant ramen, and replace the lamb with ground seitan. Add the chili crisp at the beginning of the Pre-Simmer phase and sear the seitan in it.

Replace the ground lamb with any other ground meat, such as beef or turkey.

Play with the spice mix. Try different amounts of cumin and Sichuan peppercorns, and try other spices like coriander seeds, black pepper, and star anise.

DRY AND
SAUCY

Aglio e Olio Ramen
Italian Garlic and Oil Pasta

Aglio e olio is a striking example of beauty in simplicity, a dish that hones in on its two namesake ingredients: garlic and olive oil.

I like adding olive oil at the end to create more depth of flavor—the oil retains more of its bright, vegetal flavors when it's uncooked. Using instant ramen, this classic pasta dish tastes quite different: it has a powerful umami note and the noodles have more springiness but less chew than Italian pasta.

3 Tbsp extra-virgin olive oil

3 medium garlic cloves, very thinly sliced

Pinch of red pepper flakes

¾ cup [180 ml] water

One 3 to 3½ oz [85 to 100 g] packet instant ramen

2 Tbsp finely chopped parsley

Grated Parmesan cheese, for garnish

PRE-SIMMER Heat 2 tablespoons of the oil in a saucepan over medium heat. Add the garlic and gently sauté for 2 minutes, taking care not to brown the garlic. Add the red pepper flakes and let them bloom in the oil for 15 seconds. Add the water and half of the seasoning sachet.

SIMMER Bring the water to a simmer and add the noodle cake. Because of the low water level, you'll need to jiggle and move the cake around to get the noodles to disperse. Simmer for 4 minutes or until the water has nearly fully evaporated.

FINISH Remove the saucepan from the heat. Add the parsley and remaining 1 tablespoon of oil and stir to combine. Pour the noodles onto a plate and top with Parmesan. Serve immediately.

TRY THIS For a vegetarian version, use a soy-flavored instant ramen.

For a brighter dish, at the Finish phase, add the juice of ½ a lemon along with the olive oil.

Use different combinations of leafy herbs at the Finish phase, such as basil, tarragon, cilantro, dill, or mint.

Cacio e Pepe Ramen
Italian Cheese and Black Pepper Pasta

This Italian pasta dish brings together just a few ingredients to create a creamy, peppery sauce that hits the spot. Blooming the black pepper in butter helps bring out its aromatics, putting the spotlight on an everyday spice. As is the case with other Italian-inspired recipes in this book, using instant ramen brings a level of umami savoriness that you wouldn't normally find in the dish. It's different—and delicious.

2 Tbsp unsalted butter

¼ tsp freshly ground black pepper

½ cup plus 2 Tbsp [150 ml] water

One 3 to 3½ oz [85 to 100 g] packet instant ramen

⅓ cup [20 g] grated Pecorino Romano

PRE-SIMMER Heat 1 tablespoon of the butter in a medium saucepan over medium heat. Once the butter starts foaming, add the ground pepper. Let it bloom in the butter for 15 seconds or until fragrant. Add ½ cup [120 ml] of the water and half of the seasoning sachet.

SIMMER Bring the water to a simmer and add the noodle cake. Because the water level is so low, you'll need to actively jiggle and move the noodles around to ensure even cooking. Simmer for about 3 minutes or until the water is gone. If the noodles are still too chewy, add more water.

FINISH Take the saucepan off the heat. Add the remaining 1 tablespoon of butter, the Pecorino Romano, and the remaining 2 tablespoons of water. Stir to create a sauce. Pour onto a plate and serve immediately.

TRY THIS

For a vegetarian version, use soy-flavored instant ramen.

Replace the Pecorino Romano with any hard grating cheese, such as Parmesan, Manchego, or aged Gouda.

Use other spices alongside the black pepper, such as ground cumin or red pepper flakes.

Carbonara-ish Ramen

This recipe evokes the spirit of carbonara by using a barely cooked egg and cheese to create a creamy sauce. Beyond that, admittedly, it is quite different from the traditional version (hence the *ish*). I use the dried vegetable bits as a topping to add some texture to the dish. This recipe takes about the same amount of time as it takes to make plain instant ramen and yet totally transforms its format and flavor. The only dangerous part is how easy it is to finish this bowl in just a few slurps.

1 slice American cheese

One 4½ oz [125 g] packet instant ramen

1 large egg

2 cups [475 ml] water

PRE-SIMMER In a bowl, add the cheese, half of the seasoning sachet, and the egg. Heat the water in a medium saucepan over medium-high heat.

SIMMER Bring the water to a simmer. Add the noodle cake and simmer for 3 minutes or until your desired doneness. Using the saucepan lid, drain the ramen thoroughly.

FINISH Pour the ramen into the bowl. While the noodles are still piping hot, thoroughly mix the noodles with the cheese, seasoning, and egg. The heat from the noodles will gently cook the egg. Top the ramen with the contents of the dried vegetable sachet. Serve immediately.

TRY THIS

For a dish somewhat closer to pasta carbonara, replace the American cheese with ¼ cup [10 g] or more of grated Parmesan or Pecorino Romano cheese.

For a pop of green, add a handful of baby spinach or other quick-cooking leafy vegetable near the end of the Simmer phase.

Ramen alla Marinara

This classic red sauce favorite takes on a new level of savoriness when made with instant ramen. In this recipe, the ramen noodles are cooked in a tomato broth until it has reduced to a sauce-like consistency. Because the tomato broth is acidic, it takes a bit longer to soften the noodles. Don't forget to shower the final dish with Parmesan cheese, also known by some Italian Americans as *Italian snow*.

1 Tbsp extra-virgin olive oil, plus more for garnish

2 garlic cloves, very thinly sliced

¾ cup [180 g] canned crushed or ground tomatoes

½ cup [120 ml] water

4 basil leaves, plus more for garnish

One 3 to 3½ oz [85 to 100 g] packet instant ramen

Parmesan cheese, grated, for garnish

PRE-SIMMER Heat a medium saucepan over medium heat. Add the oil and garlic. Gently cook the garlic, without browning it, for 30 seconds or until fragrant. Increase the heat to medium-high and add the tomatoes, water, basil leaves, and half of the seasoning sachet.

SIMMER Bring the liquid to a simmer. Add the noodle cake. Cook for 4 minutes, moving the noodle cake around so it breaks apart, or until the liquid has reduced to a sauce-like consistency. You may want to use a lid to prevent splattering.

FINISH Pour the noodles onto a plate. Top with a few basil leaves, a drizzle of oil, and a sprinkle of Parmesan. Serve immediately.

TRY THIS Build other tomato-based pastas out of this one. Add a generous pinch of red pepper flakes with the garlic to make an arrabbiata sauce. Add anchovies, olives, and capers to make a puttanesca sauce.

Add 1 tablespoon or more of cream at the Finish phase to make a pink sauce.

Ramen Fideuà

Catalan Noodle Paella

A traditional dish from Catalunya in the northeast of Spain, fideuà is a paella-like dish made with little noodles called *fideus*. I use crumbled-up ramen noodles to replace the fideus. Using a skillet instead of a saucepan, you can actually develop a prized part of fideuà: the socarrat, a crispy layer on the bottom that contrasts beautifully with the soft noodles above. It's a total transformation of instant ramen that will have you hooked.

2 Tbsp extra-virgin olive oil

2 garlic cloves, very thinly sliced

½ cup [120 g] canned crushed or ground tomatoes

¾ cup [180 ml] water

One 3 to 3½ oz [85 to 100 g] packet instant ramen, noodles broken into small pieces

1 tsp smoked paprika

Pinch of saffron (optional)

6 jumbo frozen shrimp (21/25 or 26/30 count)

2 Tbsp frozen peas

Chopped fresh parsley, for garnish

PRE-SIMMER Heat a 10-inch [25 cm] skillet over medium-high heat. Add the oil and garlic and let them bloom for 30 seconds or until fragrant but not burning. Add the tomatoes, water, seasoning sachet, paprika, and saffron, if using.

SIMMER Bring the soup to a gentle simmer, lowering the heat if necessary. Distribute the crumbled noodles around the skillet, ensuring they are all at least partially submerged. Nestle the shrimp into the soup and scatter the peas on top. It's important to pay attention and listen to the skillet. As the liquid evaporates, the pitch of the simmering will get higher and higher. It should start sounding dry after it has simmered for 9 minutes. Let it cook for 1 more minute to develop a browned crust on the bottom. You can use a spoon to peek around the edges to see whether the crust has developed. If you don't see a crust, keep letting it cook.

FINISH Top with parsley and serve immediately directly out of the skillet.

TRY THIS Create different flavor combinations by replacing the shrimp with other proteins, such as chorizo, and replacing the peas with other vegetables, such as diced red bell pepper.

This dish is a good canvas for artful garnishes. For example, you can add aioli or mayonnaise in a zigzag pattern; very thinly sliced vegetables, such as radishes; and other chopped herbs.

Mac 'n' Cheese Ramen

With a few ingredients and a few minutes, you can have a steaming, comforting bowl of mac 'n' cheese ramen. The key ingredient here is evaporated milk, which mimics béchamel, a creamy sauce that is usually used as the base for mac 'n' cheese. Try using high-quality, extra-sharp cheddar cheese for a particularly delicious dish.

2 cups [475 ml] water

One 3 to 3½ oz [85 to 100 g] packet instant ramen

2½ oz [70 ml] evaporated milk (half of a 5 oz [140 ml] can)

3 oz [85 g] sharp cheddar cheese, grated

SIMMER Bring the water to a simmer in a medium saucepan over medium-high heat. Add the noodle cake and cook for 2½ minutes or until your desired doneness. Drain thoroughly.

ADD the evaporated milk, cheese, and half of the seasoning sachet to the saucepan. Simmer for 1 minute to create a cheese sauce, stirring regularly.

FINISH Pour the ramen into a bowl. Serve immediately.

TRY THIS For a vegetarian version, use soy-flavored instant ramen.

Use different cheeses, such as Swiss, Gruyère, mozzarella, or Parmesan. For noodles that are closer in size to macaroni, break up the noodle cake before cooking it.

For a vegetal note, add ½ cup [70 g] of small broccoli florets during the Simmer phase. Let the broccoli simmer for 2 minutes before adding the noodle cake.

Spinach Ramen Gratin

This is the one and only baked recipe concept in the book. I mostly avoid using the oven for instant ramen in favor of speedier stovetop cooking. However, there's one thing that ovens *can* do that stovetops cannot: create a browned cheesy top. You can consider this a template for creating a gooey, cheesy instant ramen dish with an appetizing golden crust in the oven. While the overall cook time takes longer than 20 minutes, this only takes a few minutes to assemble; the rest of the time is passive.

1 cup [240 ml] milk

1 Tbsp cornstarch

⅓ cup [70 g] frozen spinach, broken up

¾ cup [60 g] shredded mozzarella

One 3½ to 4½ oz [100 to 125 g] packet instant ramen, noodle cake broken into large chunks

Preheat the oven to 400°F [200°C].

In an 8-inch [20 cm] baking dish, add the milk, cornstarch, spinach, ¼ cup [20 g] of the mozzarella, the seasoning sachet, and noodle chunks. Stir until combined, ensuring the noodle chunks are all at least partially submerged. Top with the remaining ½ cup [40 g] of mozzarella.

Bake for 20 minutes or until the cheese has browned. Serve immediately.

TRY THIS Swap out the spinach for another vegetable, such as green peas, broccoli, or tomatoes.

Add 2 to 4 ounces [55 to 115 g] of raw ground meat to the mixture.

Mix and match cheese combinations using melty cheeses, such as Gruyère; creamy ones, such as Brie; and savory ones, such as Parmesan.

B.E.C. Ramen

Bacon, Egg, and Cheese

RECOMMENDED RAMEN:
Any

If there is one breakfast item that unites New York City, it's the B.E.C. (bacon, egg, and cheese) sandwich. Wherever you are in the city, you're never far from a deli that can whip one up in a few minutes.

This recipe is an homage to a classic version of the sandwich, which you can order by saying, "Yo, I'll take a bacon-egg-and-cheese-on-a-roll-with-salt-pepper-ketchup."

---

2 strips thin-sliced bacon, cut into 1 in [2.5 cm] wide pieces

1 egg, beaten

¾ cup [180 ml] water

One 3½ to 4½ oz [100 to 125 g] packet instant ramen

1 slice American cheese

Ketchup (optional)

Ground black pepper (optional)

PRE-SIMMER Add the bacon to a cold medium saucepan and heat it over medium-high heat. Once the bacon starts sizzling, cook for 4 minutes or until most of the fat has rendered and the bacon has browned, crispy parts.

Move the bacon to the side of the saucepan and add the egg. Cook, stirring gently, until the egg has set, about 30 seconds. Break the cooked egg into large curds.

Add the water and half of the seasoning sachet.

SIMMER Bring the water to a simmer, then add the noodle cake. Since the water level is low, you'll need to jiggle and move the noodles around to ensure even cooking. Simmer the noodles for 2 minutes or until the water has evaporated.

FINISH Pour the ramen onto a plate. Top with the American cheese. If using, add ketchup in a zigzag pattern and sprinkle black pepper on top. Serve immediately.

TRY THIS   Replace the pork bacon with turkey or beef bacon, both of which are commonly used in New York City delis.

Add ½ cup [70 g] of diced vegetables, such as onions and bell peppers, with the bacon.

Finish with hot sauce.

Bibim Guksu Ramen
Korean Spicy Cold Noodle

I've eaten bibim guksu countless times with my parents. It's one of those dishes that is so refreshing and invigorating, you could eat it every day. Cool noodles get a fiery kick from gochujang and serve as a foundation for crisp, raw vegetables and pickles. The dish is highly customizable and easily flows with whatever produce is in season.

2 cups plus 1 Tbsp [490 ml] water

One 3½ to 4½ oz [100 to 125 g] packet instant ramen

1 Tbsp gochujang

1 Tbsp rice vinegar

1 tsp sesame oil

¼ medium cucumber, julienned (about ⅓ cup [40 g]), for garnish

⅓ cup [35 g] very thinly sliced cabbage, for garnish

¼ cup [35 g] sliced kimchi, for garnish

½ scallion, thinly sliced, for garnish

Roasted sesame seeds, for garnish

PRE-SIMMER Heat 2 cups [475 ml] of the water in a medium saucepan over high heat. In a bowl, combine the remaining 1 tablespoon of water, half of the seasoning sachet, the gochujang, rice vinegar, and sesame oil to make a dressing.

SIMMER Add the noodle cake to the saucepan and cook for 2½ minutes or until your desired doneness.

FINISH Drain the noodles thoroughly and rinse them in cool water until the noodles have cooled. Put the noodles in the bowl with the dressing and toss to combine. Top with the cucumber, cabbage, kimchi, scallion, and sesame seeds. Serve immediately.

TRY THIS Use other julienned or very thinly sliced vegetables, either in addition to or instead of the cucumber and cabbage.

For a non-fiery version, replace the gochujang with tahini or a nut butter.

Add a protein or a Jammy Egg (page 160).

RECOMMENDED RAMEN:
Chapagetti instant ramen

Jjajangmyeon

Korean Noodles in Black Bean Sauce

Jjajangmyeon is a beloved Korean noodle dish made with chunjang, a fermented black soybean paste, which gives it a rich, caramelly flavor. It was originally brought to Korea by Chinese immigrants and has since become a national comfort dish. Using Chapagetti instant ramen and just a few additional ingredients, you can taste for yourself why millions of Koreans crave these dark-hued savory noodles.

1 tsp neutral oil, such as sunflower oil

4 oz [115 g] ground pork

¼ medium zucchini, diced small (about ½ cup [70 g])

1 small potato, diced small (about ½ cup [70 g])

¼ cup [35 g] diced onion (about ⅛ large onion)

1¼ cups [300 ml] water

1 tsp soy sauce

1 tsp rice vinegar

One 4½ oz [125 g] packet Chapagetti instant ramen

¼ cup [40 g] julienned cucumber, for garnish

¼ cup [35 g] julienned danmuji (Korean pickled radish, optional), for garnish

PRE-SIMMER Heat the oil in a medium saucepan over high heat. Add the pork, zucchini, potato, and onion and sear for 3 minutes or until the pork has browned. Add the water.

SIMMER Once the water is simmering, let the pork and vegetables cook for 1 minute. Add the soy sauce, vinegar, and the contents of all the sachets. Add the noodle cake. You'll need to jiggle the noodle cake a fair amount to get the noodles to fully submerge. Cook for 4 minutes or until the liquid has reduced to a sauce-like consistency.

FINISH Pour the ramen into a bowl or onto a plate. Top with the cucumber and danmuji, if using. Serve immediately.

TRY THIS For a twist that I loved as a child, replace the pork with one hot dog, sliced.

Play around with the vegetable mix. Try cabbage, carrot, broccoli, peas, or other vegetables instead of the zucchini and/or the potato.

Cheesy Buldak Ramen

Korean Spicy Chicken with Cheese

Buldak (literally, "fire chicken") is a barbecued chicken dish with an intensely
fiery scarlet red sauce that is often capped with melted cheese. It inspired Buldak
instant ramen, which exploded in popularity in the 2010s thanks to viral videos that
challenged viewers to eat the noodles as quickly as possible. I don't recommend
rushing it! Take your time and savor the spicy, cheesy flavors.

1 tsp neutral oil, such as
sunflower oil

4 oz [115 g] boneless, skinless
chicken thigh (about 1 thigh),
cut into ½ in [13 mm] chunks

2¼ cups [530 ml] water

12 tteok (Korean rice cakes)

One 5 oz [140 g] packet
Buldak instant ramen

2 oz [55 g] shredded
mozzarella (about ½ cup)

1 tsp toasted sesame oil

½ scallion, thinly sliced

PRE-SIMMER Heat the neutral oil in a medium saucepan
over high heat. Sear the chicken for 3 minutes or until it has
browned all over. Add 2 cups [475 ml] of the water and the
rice cakes.

SIMMER Bring the water to a simmer. Add the noodle cake
and cook for 4 minutes or until your desired doneness. Using
the saucepan lid, drain the ramen thoroughly. Decrease the
heat to low. Add the remaining ¼ cup [60 ml] of water to the
pot. Add the Buldak sauce sachet, half of the mozzarella, and
the sesame oil and stir to combine.

FINISH Pour the ramen into a bowl. Sprinkle the remaining
mozzarella all around the top of the noodles and cover with
a plate. Let the ramen sit for 1 minute or until the cheese has
melted. Top with the scallions and the Buldak flake sachet.
Serve immediately.

TRY THIS

For a creamier version, omit
the sesame oil and add
1 tablespoon of mayonnaise
with the sauce sachet.

For a mac 'n' cheese-esque
version, omit the sesame oil,
replace the water with ¼ cup
[60 ml] of milk, and replace
the mozzarella with 3 ounces
[85 g] of shredded cheddar
cheese.

To bring some veggies into
the mix, try adding ½ cup [8 g]
or more of thinly sliced kale
while simmering.

RECOMMENDED
RAMEN:
Beef-Flavored
Classic

Sega Wat Ramen

Ethiopian Fiery Beef Stew

This recipe has only a handful of ingredients, but each one is central to Ethiopian cuisine. Berbere could be considered *the* national flavor of Ethiopia, and beef, red onions, and butter are all used extensively across the country. The result is a deliciously fiery, meaty dish that tastes unmistakably of Ethiopian culture. It packs a heavy punch—if you're sensitive to spice, I suggest dialing down the berbere a touch. I add the seasoning sachet to the onions as they cook because the salt helps break them down and caramelize faster.

1 Tbsp unsalted butter

½ cup [70 g] diced red onion (about ¼ large onion)

4 oz [115 g] ground beef

One 3 to 3½ oz [85 to 100 g] packet instant ramen

1 Tbsp berbere, plus more for garnish (optional)

¾ cup [180 ml] water

PRE-SIMMER Heat a medium saucepan over high heat. Add the butter. Once it starts foaming, add the onion, beef, and seasoning sachet. Sauté, stirring constantly, for 5 minutes or until the meat has browned and the onion has shriveled up and caramelized. Lower the heat to medium, add the berbere, and let it bloom for 15 seconds or until fragrant but not burned. Add the water and return to medium-high heat.

SIMMER Once the liquid is simmering, add the noodle cake and simmer for 3 minutes or until the liquid has reduced to a sauce-like consistency. Because the liquid level is so low, you will need to jiggle and move the noodle cake around to ensure even cooking.

FINISH Pour the ramen onto a plate. Dust with additional berbere, if desired. Serve immediately.

TRY THIS Add a halved hard-boiled or Jammy Egg (page 160) to the plate—sega wat is often traditionally served with egg.

For a dish similar to doro wat, an Ethiopian chicken stew, use chicken-flavored instant ramen and replace the beef with one boneless, skinless chicken thigh, cut into chunks.

For a fresh counterpoint to the deep flavors of this dish, add chopped herbs, such as parsley or mint, at the Finish phase.

Kare Ramen

Japanese Beef Curry Gravy

This popular Japanese comfort dish dates back to the late nineteenth century, when British sailors introduced curry powder to the cuisine. Today, the classic version includes a sweet and savory curried gravy, carrots, onions, potatoes, and beef. It's often garnished with fukujinzuke, a pickle mix made for kare, which helps balance the richness of the dish.

While this recipe only takes minutes, you'll be surprised by how much it resembles a long-simmered kare. Butter brings richness to the dish, and ketchup and apple help round it out with some sweetness and acidity. You can substitute ground beef or other tender steak cuts for the sirloin.

4 oz [115 g] sirloin, cut into ½ in [13 mm] chunks

1 Tbsp unsalted butter

1 carrot, diced small (about ⅓ cup [45 g])

½ medium Yukon gold potato, diced small (about ⅓ cup [45 g])

⅓ cup [45 g] diced red onion (about ⅛ large onion)

¼ medium apple, grated (about ⅓ cup [45 g])

One 3 to 3½ oz [85 to 100 g] packet instant ramen

2 Tbsp ketchup

2 Tbsp all-purpose flour

1 Tbsp curry powder

1½ cups [360 ml] water

Fukujinzuke, or other pickle, for garnish (optional)

PRE-SIMMER Heat a medium saucepan over high heat. Add the sirloin, butter, carrot, potato, onion, apple, and seasoning sachet. Stirring frequently, sauté for 4 minutes or until the beef has browned and the vegetables have softened.

Add the ketchup, flour, and curry powder. Sauté for 30 seconds, stirring to combine all the ingredients. Add the water. Scrape up any stuck browned bits from the saucepan.

SIMMER Once the soup has started simmering, it will begin to thicken. Add the noodle cake. Stirring frequently to prevent sticking, simmer for 3 minutes or until the liquid has reached a thick gravy-like consistency.

FINISH Pour the ramen into a bowl. If using, top with a small mound of pickles. Serve immediately.

TRY THIS   Use different combinations of proteins and vegetables, maintaining the same overall quantities. For example, try chicken, tofu, or shrimp instead of beef. Try daikon, cabbage, cauliflower, peas, or corn as vegetables.

If you'd like to have the noodles separate from the gravy, decrease the water by ½ cup [120 ml] and cook the noodles in a separate saucepan. For a classic presentation, plate the noodles first, and then partially cover the noodles with the gravy.

For a kare with a kick, add red pepper flakes to your desired level of fieriness with the curry powder.

Acknowledgments

This cookbook is my first. It's not only a milestone in my career in food culture and storytelling; it's also a reflection of my own life philosophies, which value creativity, playfulness, unabashed self-expression, accessibility, and openness. I'd like to recognize just a few among many souls who have shaped me and, by extension, this book.

Ok Joo Cho, my halmoni, whose bravery and resilience made everything possible.

Young Ja Kim, my mother, for giving me emotional security and the ability to dream.

Hong Chun Kim, my father, for giving me your intense passion and focus.

Andrew Kim, my brother, for inspiring a lifelong pursuit of food. When I was a wee kid in the cornfields of Illinois, you made a pesto chicken dish that I'll never forget. The flavors awakened my interest in cooking.

Félix and Olive, my little dumplings, for being my favorite taste testers and making my heart swell each day anew. I'll always be willing to fire up a pot of ramen just to see those beautiful smiles on your faces.

Stéphanie Jacquemont, for bringing the little dumplings into the world and being their loving mother.

Valentina Bernal Ibague, for never tiring of my constant ramen cookery and for your daily support.

Maddy Wong, for initiating this journey and being an extra-ordinary partner, always thoughtful, gracious, and open to new ideas. We pivoted from pizza to instant ramen without skipping a beat.

Chronicle Books, for taking a chance on a most unusual concept.

David Black, for shepherding me through the process and for encouraging me to bring my personal voice into the narrative.

Harold McGee, for creating that first spark of curiosity that blossomed into an obsession with food culture and science. It's a pleasure to have gotten to know you first through your writing and then, decades later, as a friend and advisor.

Jessica B. Harris, for being my North Star when it comes to integrity, excellence, and poetry in food storytelling. It has been an honor of a lifetime to learn from you and do my best to keep up.

Nastassia Lopez, for always being there to laugh at the good times . . . and laugh even harder at the bad times.

Emma Boast, for being my copilot in creating the Museum of Food and Drink, a process that formed the blueprint for my own personal perspective on food and drink.

Coral Lee and Harry Sultan, for diving with me into an irreverent romp through food, music, and culture. (Listen to our podcast *Counterjam* to hear the results.)

Francis Lam, for the early advice on the ins and outs of cookbook proposals.

All the culinary industry friends who have expanded my understanding of food and drink culture, including Einat Admony, Ted Allen, Dominique Ansel, Michael Anthony, Dave Arnold, Scott Barton, Marco Canora, Cesare Casella, David Chang, Maneet Chauhan, Adrienne Cheatham, Chris Cheung, Roy Choi, Amanda Cohen, Dana Cowin, Kia Damon, Wylie Dufresne, Elizabeth Falkner, Carolina Gelen, Daniel Gritzer, Alex Guarnaschelli, Carla Hall, Amanda Hesser, Tonya Hopkins, John Hutt, Mark Ladner, Jim Lahey, Mike Lee, Anita Lo, Kenji López-Alt, Jean Nihoul, Garrett Oliver, Enrique Olvera, Dan Pashman, Jeff Porter, Alex Raij, Jordana Rothman, Adam Sachs, Marcus Samuelsson, Rich Shih, Bryce Shuman, Sheldon Simeon, Gail Simmons, Lucas Sin, Alexander Smalls, Peter Som, Dale Talde, Omar Tate, Nicole Taylor, Bill Telepan, Pierre Thiam, Michael Twitty, Anna Voloshyna, Jonathan Wu, Bill Yosses, and Andrew Zimmern.

All the artists, creatives, and musicians who have nurtured my creative renaissance over the past couple years, including El Atigh Abba, Lana Bakour, Steven Balasta, Vikram Bhaskaran, Lila Bloom, Nick Boni, Paul Bourque, Ben Bourque, Bruna Braga, Mireia Clua, Nick Coleman, Tiffany Comprès, Flavie Denoyelle, Josh Finn, Georges Janin, Julia Lessa, Richard Lowenburg, Sam Lowenburg, Al Malonga, Amber Mazor, Adriana Merenda, Nyneve Minnear, Natalia Perez, David Reed, Oscar Riquelme, Divan Shamshtein, Emilio Tamburini, and Naveen Thomas.

Index

Chronicle Books publishes distinctive books and gifts. From award-winning children's titles, bestselling cookbooks, and eclectic pop culture to acclaimed works of art and design, stationery, and journals, we craft publishing that's instantly recognizable for its spirit and creativity. Enjoy our publishing and become part of our community at www.chroniclebooks.com.